THE CARD CONNECTION

131 quick & easy handmade cards for all occasions!

How very special we feel when opening a card. Yes, even with e-mail and cell phones, receiving a card is heartwarming. If that card is handmade, the connection is even more perfect.

Now, creating handmade cards is easier than ever! Because now you have hundreds of wonderful accents to use, right at your fingertips. They are found in The Card Connection at your local Michaels Arts & Crafts Store. This comprehensive collection includes many delightful, finished pieces, along with many decorative accents, to be used in cardmaking. Simply decorate your blank card with papers, eyelets, cording or ribbon, then add the prefinished accent for the perfect handmade card!

The Card Connection is filled with hundreds of versatile components, designed to be used on cards to celebrate friendships, weddings, new babies, birthdays and all other celebrations. In addition, you'll find a special message collection, along with buttons, beads, eyelets, wire, metal, threads and all the blank cards and envelopes you'll ever need! This innovative collection of wonderful components is brought to you by Hirschberg Schutz and Michaels Stores, Inc. Brenda Lugannani, Anita Carter and all the people involved in bringing The Card Connection to you hope you're inspired to create wonderful, heartfelt greetings!

Production Credits

President: Paulette Jarvey
Vice-President: Teresa Nelson
Production Manager: Lynda Hill
Editors: Paulette Jarvey, Lynda Hill
Project Editor: India Mayo
Photographer: John McNally
Graphic Designers: Jacie Pete, Joy Schaber
Digital Imagers: Victoria Weber, Scott Gordon

Table of Contents

Tools

Adhesives: There are several options when working with papers:

E-6000®—heavy duty adhesive that adheres metals, glass, beads, plastic and wood to projects.

Foam adhesive tape—double-sided adhesive foam. It adheres pieces together while raising them off the background; use mulitple layers for more lift. Available in strips or dots.

Mono Adhesive™—liquid glue in a bottle which dispenses in a thick or thin line. Excellent for gluing papers together.

Stick glue—easy, convenient and secure.

Terrifically Tacky Tape™—double-sided adhesive tape used to adhere small beads, tinsel and glitter to objects.

Decorative Scissors have blades which are shaped into different edge styles.

Eyelet Tools are necessary to attach eyelets to paper. The tools include a universal hole punch, an eyelet-setting tool and a hammer. (See page 5 for instructions for attaching eyelets.)

Paper Punches are small tools which cut different shapes from paper. They are available in small and large single shapes, border and corner configurations and with long handles to reach further. There are many styles from which to choose.

Pens with permanent pigment inks are best as they dry quickly and do not run. A myriad of colors are available to color coordinate with your cards.

Ruler: The best ruler is metal with a cork backing. The metal eliminates the possibility of slicing off a piece of the ruler when using your craft knife and the backing raises the metal off the cardstock to prevent your pen from bleeding under it.

A Self-healing Cutting Mat or Cutting Board is essential when using a craft knife and ruler to cut paper and cardstock.

An X-acto® or Craft Knife is best when used with a metal ruler and cutting mat. The knife makes very clean, straight cuts. For best results, be sure to change your blades often!

Materials

Card Connection Embellishments—all the embellishments are sold in packages. In the projects we refer to them as "packs" (see inside the back cover).

Cardstock—plain colored, heavy-weight paper used in making cards. Available folded into blank cards in varying sizes and colors. Flat sheet cardstock is also available.

Corrugated Paper—heavy paper that has a rippled side and a flat side; the rippled side is the decorative side.

Decorative or Patterned Paper—sheets of paper which have a pattern printed on one side. They are purchased by the sheet or in books of coordinating designs.

Micro Beads or Tiny Glass Marbles—very tiny colored beads which have no holes; they add a glistening effect.

Seed Beads—tiny 2mm-4mm glass beads with holes, available in many colors and styles; they can be stitched, wired or glued to a card in patterns as embellishments.

Vellum—translucent paper available in varying colors and patterns; it's used to enhance cards when cut into shapes or used for lettering messages.

Techniques

Covering a Card—apply glue to the card. Position the paper and smooth in place. Turn the card over and trim off the excess paper.

Cutting—for straight edges, a craft knife, rulers and cutting mat work the best. For curved lines, sharp scissors are the easiest, and for small areas, small scissors make it easy to cut the details.

Eyelets—use the universal hole punch and with a hammer punch a hole in the paper where you want the eyelet located. Insert the eyelet through the hole, front to back, then turn the paper and eyelet over. Place the eyelet setter over the back of the eyelet and pound the setter with the hammer to secure.

Lettering—hand lettering on your cards can be tricky; we suggest lettering on a separate piece of paper, then trimming and gluing it to the card. Using a computer and printer can make lettering even easier, even on vellum, especially with all the fun and fancy fonts available today.

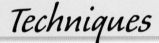

Matting—glue the object to be matted onto paper. Cut around it, following its shape while leaving the specified border of matting paper around the edges.

Scoring—pressing a scoring line into a card makes folding it much easier and neater. To score, place your card or paper on the table and position the straight edge of your ruler where you want the scored line to be. Use the dull side of an X-acto® knife to press into the paper along the ruler's edge.

Tearing Papers and Cardstock—torn edges add depth and interest to cards and paper embellishments on cards. *For a straight edge,* firmly hold a metal ruler on the paper with the edge aligned where it's to be torn; pull the paper upward toward you, tearing along the edge of the ruler. *For uneven torn edges,* hold the paper and tear, being careful to tear it to the approximate sized needed. If tearing around a design or art, be sure to begin tearing far enough away from the edge of the art to prevent a stray tear from entering into the art area.

Transferring Patterns—trace the pattern onto tracing paper and cut out. Lay it on the paper, trace around it then cut it from the paper.

Birthday Connections

The happiest birthday celebrations are those which include cards from friends and loved ones. And the best cards are those which are made by hand with the birthday celebrant in mind!

Rhinestone cupcakes, party hats, stacked gifts and laser-cut messages are embellishments that make creating special cards easy. They become great focals when creating impressive, one-of-a-kind birthday greetings. Celebrate your loved ones' birthdays with beautiful cards that will become treasures—made by you!

Red Hat for Mom
by Jeanne Jacobowski

4"x5¼" ivory card
red hat & stand with tag pack
solid papers: black moiré, metallic gold/black
gold splattered vellum
two ¼" round red rhinestones
optional: Sizzix machine and scalloped frame
    die-cut #38-0306
decorative scissors: deckle, cloud

1. With the fold on the left, trim the front and back right edges of the card with the deckle scissors. Cut a piece of black moiré the same size as the unfolded card, fold in half and trim the right edges with the deckle scissors. Glue the ivory card inside the black card.

2. Cut a 7½"x5" piece of metallic gold/black paper. Fold in half and trim the right edges with the deckle scissors. Glue to the outside of the black card.

3. Use the Sizzix and die-cut to cut the frame from moiré paper. Or use the pattern to cut the oval from moiré then trim the edges with the cloud scissors. Cut and glue a piece of vellum to fit behind the frame. Glue it to the card front then glue the red hat in the center of the frame.

4. Glue the rhinestones on the left front of the card, ⅛" from the fold and 1" from the top and bottom.

5. Cut a 5"x3¾" piece of gold splattered vellum. Glue the left edge inside the card and trim the right edge with the deckle scissors.

Angel Birthday Card
by Susan Cobb

5"x7¼" white card
pink girl angel pack
patterned papers: pink/white
    tri-dot, pink/green/blue plaid
    (from the book Paper Pizazz™
    Baby's First Year)
light green paper
four ³⁄₁₆" dark pink eyelets
10" of ¼" wide sheer pink
    ribbon with silver thread pack
metallic silver thread
X-acto® knife, cutting surface
silver pen, ruler

1. Cut a 4⅞"x7" piece of tri-dot paper and glue centered on the card front. Cut a 4¼"x6½" piece of plaid paper and glue centered on the tri-dot paper. Cut a 2⅞"x4" piece of tri-dot paper and glue to the plaid paper ¾" from the top.

2. Open the card and cut a 2¼"x3 window from the center of the small tri-dot rectangle. Cover the inside of the card with light green paper. Use the silver pen to outline all the tri-dot pieces and add scallops.

3. Insert one eyelet in each corner of the tri-dot window frame. Thread four strands of 8" long silver thread through the top two eyelets. Tie inside to secure. Repeat for the bottom eyelets, except tie tightly. Glue the angel to the center of the top thread.

4. Cut a ¾"x3" piece of light green paper and mat on tri-dot leaving a ¹⁄₁₆" border. Write the message with the silver pen then glue centered below the window. Tie a shoestring bow with the pink ribbon and glue as shown.

Birthday Doll Card
by Susan Cobb

5"x7¼" white card
Happy Birthday doll pack
dark pink floral handmade paper
solid metallic silver paper (from the book Paper Pizazz™
*   Metallic Silver, also by the sheet)*
pink vellum (from the book Paper Pizazz™ 12"x12" Pastel
*   Vellum Papers, also by the sheet)*

1 Cut a 5"x7" piece of handmade paper and glue it centered on the card front.

2 Cut a 2½"x3½" piece of silver paper and mat it on pink vellum with a ⅛" border. Attach the doll centered on the silver paper. Glue the vellum centered on the card front.

Hat Boxes Birthday Card
by Susan Cobb

5"x7⅛" white card
sequined butterfly birthday pack
metallic silver bow pack
patterned papers: lavender gingham (from the book Paper
*   Pizazz™ Soft Tints)*
pastel purple vellum (from the book Paper Pizazz™ 12"x12"
*   Pastel Vellum Papers, also by the sheet)*
white handmade paper with silver glitter pattern

1 Cut a 4¾"x7" piece of lavender gingham paper and glue flush with the card top and centered on the remaining sides. Cut a 3"x6½" piece of handmade paper. Score a line 1" from the top, fold and glue the flap centered on the back of the card front.

2 Cut a 3"x2" piece of vellum and glue it across the center of the handmade paper.

3 Attach the butterfly, present and "Happy Birthday" to the vellum as shown. Glue the silver bow to the upper left corner of the vellum.

It's Your Day to be Queen
by Lisa Garcia-Bergstedt

5"x7¼" white card
tiara pack
gold tassel pack
solid papers: pink, white, blue
patterned papers: pink swirl, blue dots (from the book Paper Pizazz™ Bright Tints)
eyelets: two ¼" gold, four ³/₁₆" gold
black pen

1 Trim the card to 5" square. Open the card flat and fold each side into the center fold making a tri-panel card.

2 Cut a 4¾" square of blue dots paper and glue it to the inside center of the card. Cut a 4" square of white paper and mat on pink with a ¹/₁₆" border. Glue to the center of the blue dots paper. Attach one ³/₁₆" eyelet to each corner. Glue the tiara to the center and write your message with the black pen.

3 Cut a 4¾" square of pink swirl and cut it in half. Glue one half to each front flap so the edges meet at the opening. Attach one ¼" eyelet to each flap as shown and thread the tassel through.

4 Write the message on white paper and mat on blue with a ¹/₁₆" border. Attach to the flaps.

inside card

Burgundy Bouquet
by Jeanne Jacobowski

5¾"x8¾" white card
Happy Birthday bouquet pack
lavender tag & ribbon pack
burgundy paper
patterned papers: lavender texture, lavender words (from the book Paper Pizazz™ Joy's Vintage Papers)
black pen

1 Cover the card front with lavender texture paper. Cut a 4½"x7⅝" piece of words paper and mat it on burgundy, leaving a ⅛" border. Glue it centered on the card front.

2 Glue the bouquet just above the center of the card and let dry. Write "Happy Birthday" on the tag with the black pen. Tie it to the bouquet with the ribbon.

Sweet Sixteen

by Susan Cobb

5"x7⅛" white card
sweet swirls & ice cream birthday pack
handmade paper pack
pink swirls patterned paper (from the book Paper Pizazz™ Soft Tints)
pink vellum (from the book Paper Pizazz™ 12"x12" Pastel Vellum Papers)
white sticker letters
foam adhesive tape

1 Cover the card front with pink swirls paper. Cut a 3¼" pink vellum square and turn on point as shown. Glue it centered on the card front. Cut a 3" square of white handmade paper and glue it to the vellum as shown.

2 Attach the birthday pieces to the center of the handmade paper square as shown.

3 Cut a 1"x5" pink vellum strip and glue it across the bottom of the card front. Add the message to the vellum strip with the sticker letters.

Pocket Power

by Lisa Garcia-Bergstedt

5¼"x7⅛" white card
box with butterflies pack
confetti paper (from the book Paper Pizazz™ A Girl's Scrapbook)
four ³⁄₁₆" silver eyelets
silver wire
round toothpick or skewer
foam adhesive tape

1 Cut a 4¾"x6½" piece of confetti paper. Attach it to the card front with an eyelet in each corner.

2 Cut three 3" lengths of wire and wrap around a toothpick. Slip off and repeat with the other wires. Attach one butterfly to each coil then glue them and the box to the card front as shown.

3 Cut four 4"–5" lengths of wire. Insert one end of a wire from the back of an eyelet, leaving ¼" length taped to the back. Coil the remaining wire on the card front. Repeat for the three remaining eyelets.

Celebrate!
by Donna Smith

5¼" square white card
candles sticker pack
solid papers: pink, yellow, light blue, white
¼" hole punch
black pen

1 Trim the card to 5" square.

2 To make the window flap: Mark a square in the center of the card 1" from each side. Cut through the card front on the two sides and bottom of the flap and score the top.

3 Glue the front of the card to the back everywhere except for the flap.

4 Punch eight yellow circles, 10 pink circles and eight blue circles. Attach to the border around the flap.

5 Cut a 2⅜" white square. Mat on pink with a ¹⁄₁₆" border. Repeat matting on yellow, then blue with a ¹⁄₁₆"-⅛" border. Glue to the flap with the candles in the center.

6 Cut a 5¼" square of pink paper and attach to the back of the card. Write "Celebrate" under the candles with the black pen.

Congratulations!
by Jeanne Jacobowski

5¾"x8¾" silver card
Congratulations!, cupcake, party hat pack
rhinestone flowers pack
lavender paper
patterned papers: hearts/flowers, beige speckles (from the book Paper Pizazz™ Lisa Williams Pink, Lavender & Beige)
pink vellum (from the book Paper Pizazz™ Pastel Vellum Papers)
twelve ³⁄₁₆" silver eyelets
pink cording
deckle decorative scissors

1 Trim the edges of the silver card with the deckle scissors.

2 Cut a 5½"x8½" piece of hearts/flower paper and glue it to the card front as shown. Attach an eyelet in each corner.

3 Cut a 4"x5¹⁄₁₆" piece of speckled paper and mat on lavender paper leaving a ⅛" mat. Attach an eyelet in each corner. Tear a 2¾"x 3¾" piece of vellum and attach it centered on the speckles paper with an eyelet in each corner. Glue it centered on the hearts/flowers paper.

4 Attach the Congratulations! banner, cupcake, party hat and rhinestones as shown.

5 Thread lengths of cord through the eyelets, securing them to the inside of the card.

Fans
by Susan Cobb

5"x6½" white card
fan pack
tassel pack
specialty papers: gold/black tiles, solid gold (from the book
** Paper Pizazz™ Metallic Gold)**
black paper

1 Cover the card front with black paper. Cut a 4¼"x5¾" piece of tiles paper and mat it on a gold leaving a torn border as shown. Glue it centered on the card front.

2 Glue the fans to the card front as shown. Apply glue to the gold fan, then attach a red tassel as shown.

Silver & Blue Collage
by Susan Cobb

5"x7⅛" silver card
birthday stickers pack
gifts pack
metallic patterned papers: light blue/
** silver stripe, light blue/silver tiles,**
** solid metallic silver (from the book**
** Paper Pizazz™ Metallic Silver)**
pastel blue vellum

1 With the card fold at the top glue a 4"x4¾" of stripe paper to the left side of the card even with the bottom edge. Cut a 5½"x4" piece of tiles paper and glue it horizontally overlapping the stripe paper leaving a ½" silver border on the right and bottom of the card.

2 Cut a 4¾"x2" piece of solid silver paper and glue to the center of the tiles paper. Cut a 1"x6½" strip of stripe paper with blue stripes at each edge. Glue over the center as shown. Cut a 3" square of vellum and glue it 1¼" from the right edge of the card, centered over the silver rectangle.

3 Glue the blue & white gift to the center of the card. Mat the "Happy Birthday" sticker on silver leaving a ⅛" border, then glue it to the card front as shown.

Pink Vellum Jacket
by Susan Cobb

5¼" square white card
"Best Wishes" laser cut message
pink sheer ribbon flowers with beaded centers pack
patterned papers: pink stripe, pink roses (from the
*   book Paper Pizazz™ Soft Florals & Patterns)*
pastel pink vellum
silver pen

1 With the fold at the top cover the card front with stripe paper. Cut a 4½" square of roses paper and glue to the center of the stripe paper.

2 For the triangular flaps: Cut a 12"x6" piece of pink vellum and place the card in the center. Crease a fold in the vellum ½" above and below the top and bottom edges of the card, folding the vellum to overlap the card front. Unfold and remove the card. On one short edge of the vellum, mark the center point. Using a ruler, make a line from the corner of the crease to the center point on the short edge. Repeat for the other short edge. Cut along the lines. Repeat on the other vellum short edge.

3 Glue the card in the center of the vellum. Use the silver pen to outline the edges of the vellum flaps and the roses paper. Center the "Best Wishes" greeting over the tips of the flaps then glue it only to the top flap, letting it overlap the bottom flap. Glue a flower above the greeting and the other below so the greeting will tuck behind the flower. Write the message with the silver pen.

Party Hat
by Donna Smith

5"x7" white card
party hat pack
primary cording pack
confetti patterned paper (from the book Paper Pizazz™
*   Our Holidays & Seasons)*
solid papers: red, blue, green
four 7/16" yellow buttons

1 Cover the card front with red paper. Cut a 4⅝"x6⅝" piece of blue paper and glue it centered on the card. Cut a 2¾"x4" piece of confetti paper and mat it on green leaving a ¼" border. Attach the party hat sticker centered on the confetti paper.

2 Thread red cording through the buttons, gluing one to each corner as shown.

Wishes
by Susan Cobb

5"x6½" white card
metallic embossed stars pack
phrases sticker pack
gold/black stripe patterned paper (from the book
    Paper Pizazz™ Metallic Gold)
black paper
gold eyelash fiber
foam adhesive tape
X-acto® knife, ruler, cutting surface

1 Cover the card front with stripe paper. Cover the inside with black paper.

2 Open the card face up on your cutting surface. Use your ruler and X-acto® knife to cut a 1½" square window 1¾" from the top edge of the card front.

3 Attach an embossed star to the inside back, centered in the window. Glue a 6½" length of fiber to the card as shown.

4 Mat the words sticker to gold paper, then on black leaving a narrow border. Glue it centered below the window.

Happy Birthday
by LeNae Gerig

5"x6½" white card
Happy Birthday gift pack
blue dots patterned paper (from the book
    Paper Pizazz™ Bright Tints)
solid papers: yellow, white
blue eyelets
foam adhesive tape

1 Cut a 6¼"x4¾" piece of blue dots paper and glue it centered on the card front.

2 Cut a 4¼"x2⅛" piece of white and mat it on yellow with a ⅛" border. Adhere the "Happy Birthday" sticker to the center as shown.

3 Cut a ½"x6½" strip of white and attach it to the card front with an eyelet in each end. Attach the matted sticker with foam tape as shown.

4 Cut three 1¾" white squares and mat each on yellow with a 1/16" border. Attach the stickers to the squares as shown. Attach the squares to the card evenly spaced with foam tape.

Happy Birthday
by LeNae Gerig

5"x7⅛" white card
suit pack
happy birthday pack
solid papers: white, black, medium blue
blue diamond patterned paper (from the book Paper
  Pizazz™ Soft Florals & Patterns)
alphabet tiles (from the book Paper Pizazz™ Alphabet Tiles
black eyelets
foam adhesive tape

1 Trim the card to 5" square. Cover the card front with diamonds paper. Tear a 2" wide strip of blue paper. With the card fold on the left, glue the strip to the left side of the card. Trim the paper even with the card.

2 Cut a 2⅜"x3¼" piece of white paper and mat it on black leaving a ¹⁄₁₆" border. Attach the suit to the rectangle, then attach it with foam tape to the card front as shown.

3 Cut a ¾"x2½" white rectangle and mat it on black leaving a ¹⁄₁₆" border. Attach it centered below the suit with an eyelet in each end. Attach "Happy Birthday" to the center. Cut out the desired alphabet tiles and attach them to the right side of the card with foam tape.

Special Wishes
Susan Cobb

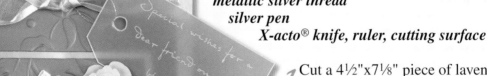

5"x7⅛" silver card
birthday cake, flower and card pack
metallic silver paper (from the book Paper
  Pizazz™ Metallic Silver)
floral metallic lavender embossed paper
lavender vellum tag
13" of ⅞" wide sheer lavender ribbon with
  satin edge
metallic silver thread
  silver pen
  X-acto® knife, ruler, cutting surface

inside

1 Cut a 4½"x7⅛" piece of lavender embossed paper. Fold the top back ¼" and place on a cutting surface. With an X-acto® and ruler, cut a 3½" square from the center of the paper, 1½" from the bottom. Place the fold over the top of the card front and glue. Glue the bottom corners of the lavender paper to the card front. Cover the inside back of the card with metallic lavender embossed paper.

2 Open the card and lay face up on the cutting surface. Cut a 3¼" square from the silver card front only, inside the lavender square. Slip the ribbon under the lavender paper at the top of the card front, tie in a knot as shown and secure with glue. Write the message on the tag with the silver pen and tie it to the ribbon with the silver thread. Glue the birthday cake, flower and card to the card inside so they show through the window.

Rhinestone Cake

by Kelly Woodard

5"x7⅛" yellow card
rhinestone birthday cake pack
Bob Hope birthday message
solid papers: purple, orange, yellow, maroon, red
sunflower decorative scissors
foam adhesive tape

1 Cut purple paper 1" smaller than the card and trim with the sunflower scissors. Glue centered on the card.

2 Cut each flame shape using the patterns on page 80 with the sunflower scissors. For more impact, attach the pieces with foam tape starting with the largest piece in the back.

3 Cut a 4½"x1" piece of orange and glue it to the card as shown. Glue the message to it.

4 Use foam tape to build the cake up to the same height as the flames and attach to the card overlapping the flames.

Happy Birthday Tag

by Lisa Garcia-Bergstedt

5"x7⅛" red card
boy/girl/children pack
green tag pack
primary stripe patterned paper (from the book Paper Pizazz™ A Girl's Scrapbook)
solid paper: black
four ³⁄₁₆" black eyelets
lemon Twistel™
black pen
foam adhesive tape

1 Cut a 4⅝"x6⅞" piece of stripe paper. Mat onto black paper with a ⅛" border. Attach centered on the card using one black eyelet in each corner.

2 Glue the tag to the card front as shown. Tie an 8" length of Twistel™ into a shoestring bow and glue to the tag.

3 Add the message with the black pen then glue the boy and children to the tag.

Sparkle Cupcake
by Jeanne Jacobowski

5"x6½" white card
sparkle cupcake pack
patterned papers: green diamonds, fuchsia
  diamonds (from the book Paper Pizazz™ A Girl's
  Scrapbook)
solid papers: light blue, blue
eyelets: 8 lime green, 8 fuchsia
foam adhesive tape

1 Trim the card to 5" square. Cut two 2⅛" squares of fuchsia diamonds paper, two 2⅛" squares of green diamonds and one 2¼" square of light blue paper.

2 Mat each square on blue paper leaving a ⅟16" border on each.

3 With the fold of the card at the top glue the fuchsia and green diamonds squares on the front as shown. Open the card and attach the eyelets to the outside corners of the squares as shown.

4 Attach the eyelets in the corners of the blue square as shown. Attach it centered on the card with foam tape. Glue the cupcake in the center of the square.

Picture Frame
by Jackie Jernstrom

5"x6½" white card
framed picture pack
square rhinestones pack
collage paper pack
primary ribbons pack

metallic silver paper (from the book
  Paper Pizazz™ Metallic Silver)
lavender paper (from the book
  Paper Pizazz™ Solid Muted
  Colors)

1 Cover the front of the card with handmade paper. Wrap the ribbon around the card as shown, gluing the ends behind the handmade paper.

2 Attach the picture frame to the card front over the ribbon. Tie the remaining ribbon into a bow and glue it to the card as shown. Attach the large rhinestone to the ribbon.

3 Journal "Happy Birthday" on lavender paper and mat each on silver leaving a ⅟16" border. Glue them to the card as shown. Attach the two small rhinestones.

4 Cut a 5⅛"x6¾" piece of silver and glue to the back of the card.

Celebration Connections

Congratulations...Lynn

dance, dance, dance!

Special life events are made even more extraordinary when celebrated with handmade cards. Large or small, share those celebrations with loved ones using your creative ideas and make a card to honor the moment. Coordinating papers with embellishments to create your card is fun and allows you to tailor your message to the recipient.

Use the ideas shown here as a beginning point to creating your unique message, changing the elements or words to match your life event. Celebrate the move to a new home, the success of a musical recital, or a simple moment of togetherness is easy—and these marvelous cards become special treasures!

Presents "Z" Fold

by Donna Smith

4"x5¼" ivory card
fancy gifts & tag pack
solid papers: gold, pink, ivory
deckle decorative scissors
foam adhesive tape

1 For the "Z" fold: Fold the right edge of the card front onto itself so the right edge meets the fold.

2 Cut a 2¾" square of gold and trim the edge with the deckle scissors. Cut a 2¼" square of pink and glue centered on the gold. Cut a 2⅛" square of ivory and glue centered on the pink.

3 Glue the left half of the layered square to the folded back card as shown, leaving the other half unglued.

4 Attach the gift packages to the square using one layer of foam tape for two of the packages, and two layers for the center present. Glue the tag to the gift as shown.

Picture Frame

by LeNae Gerig

5"x6½" white card
gold frame pack
sheer bow pack
sheer ribbon pack
patterned papers: yellow handmade-look paper, yellow handmade-look vellum (from the book Paper Pizazz™ Flowered "Handmade" Papers & Vellum)
white paper
photograph
brown decorating chalk

1 Cover the card front with handmade-look paper. Tear a 2½" wide strip of vellum and glue it centered on the card as shown. Trim the ends even with the card.

2 Glue a length of sheer tan ribbon down the center of the vellum. Tear a 2½" white square and chalk the edges. Glue it over the ribbon as shown.

3 If necessary, trim the photo to fit inside the frame. Glue the frame to the white square, then glue the bow to the frame as shown.

Saxophone and Music Notes
by Donna Smith

4"x5¼" white card
gold saxophone and music notes pack
solid papers: red, black, gold patterned, white with gold/
*   silver flecks*
gold sheet music vellum
foam adhesive tape

1 With the fold on the left side, trim ⅛" from the long edge of the card front.

2 Cut a 3⅞"x5¼" piece of vellum and glue only the left edge to the card front even with the fold.

3 Cut a ¼"x5¼" piece of black and glue it to the right edge inside the card.

4 Cut a 1¾"x5¼" piece of black and glue over the vellum next to the fold. Cut a 1½"x5¼" piece of red and glue centered on the black. Cut a 1⅜"x5¼" piece of gold patterned paper and glue centered on the red. Cut a 1¼"x5¼" piece of gold/silver flecks paper and glue centered on the gold.

5 Attach the saxophone, music notes and sequins as shown using foam tape.

Dad
by LeNae Gerig

5"x6½" white card
tools pack
red/black buffalo check patterned paper (from
*   the book Paper Pizazz™ Great Outdoors,*
*   also by the sheet)*
solid papers: tan, black
alphabet tags (from the book Paper Pizazz™
*   Tag Art)*
black eyelets

1 Trim the card to 5" square. With the fold at the top, cover the card front with check paper.

2 Tear a 2½" wide strip of black paper and a 1½" wide strip of tan paper. Layer them together as shown and attach them to the card front with an eyelet in each end. Trim the ends even with the card.

3 Cut out the alphabet tags and attach them to the card front with eyelets. Glue the tools to the card as shown.

Balloons
by LeNae Gerig

5"x6½" white card
balloons pack
striped patterned paper (from the book Paper
Pizazz™ Childhood Memories)
solid papers: white, red, yellow
white vellum
foam adhesive tape

1 Cover the card with stripe paper. Tear a 2¾" wide strip of yellow paper and glue it to the right side as shown. Trim the edges even with the card.

2 Cut a 2½"x2¾" piece of white paper and mat it on red leaving a ⅛" border. Attach it with foam tape to the card front as shown. Attach the balloons to the white paper.

3 Journal a message on white vellum and attach it to the card front with an eyelet in each end.

Dance, Dance, Dance
by Jeanne Jacobowski

5¾"x8¾" white card
ballerina, hanger & slippers pack
paper: silver, pink embossed
white dot vellum
9/16" wide pink satin ribbon pack
clear micro beads
sticker letters: pink, silver
¼" hole punch
scallop decorative scissors
7½" of ⅛" wide stick
Terrifically Tacky Tape

1 Cut the pink paper and the white vellum to 8½"x5¼". Trim both pieces at the same time with the scallop scissors. Center the two pieces on the front of the card.

2 Lay a 9" length of ribbon ¼" from the fold. Glue four areas of the ribbon to the card. Put a strip of tacky tape at each spot and cover with micro beads. Trim the ribbon ends at an angle.

3 Cut a 5¾"x3¾" piece of silver paper and glue centered on the card front. Lay a strip of tacky tape around all four edges of the silver paper. Place the card on a cookie sheet or something to contain the beads. Pour the beads onto the card to cover the tacky tape. Push them into the tape to secure. Repeat until all of the tape is covered.

4 Glue the stick slightly below center with tacky tape over each end. Cover the tape with beads.

5 Glue the ballerina outfit and slippers as shown. Add the message with the sticker letters.

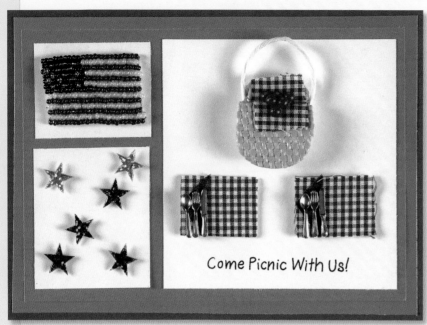

Independence Picnic
by Donna Smith

**5"x7⅛" silver card
picnic pack
flag and stars pack
solid papers: white, blue, red
silver paper (from the book Paper Pizazz™
   Metallic Silver)**

1 Cut a 4⅝"x6¾" piece of blue and glue centered on the card front.

2 Cut three pieces of white: 4⅛"x4¼", 2"x2⅜" and 2"x1⅝" and glue to the blue as shown.

3 Glue the picnic pieces, flag and stars as shown.

4 Cut a 7⅜"x5¼" piece of red and glue to the back of the card.

Music Notes
by LeNae Gerig

**5"x6½" white card
sheet music paper pack
piano pack
burgundy cardstock
black eyelets**

1 Cut a 4⅜"x5½" piece of sheet music paper and mat it on burgundy with a ⅛" border. Glue it centered on the card front.

2 Glue the piano and bench to the left side of the sheet music paper as shown.

3 Journal "Piano Recital" on burgundy. Tear the top and edges so the strip is 1" wide. Attach it to the card front with an eyelet in each end, trimming the ends even with the card.

Movie Pop-up Invitation

by Jeanne Jacobowski

5"x7⅛" red card
popcorn & beer multi-pack
vellum: blue, white swirl, white stripe
paper: gold, ivory wide stripe
ivory cardstock
star rhinestones
blue sticker letters
craft foam: red, white
⅛" off-white beads
¼" hole punch
decorative scissors: deckle, cloud
pop dots

Note: When gluing on the three-dimensional pieces–such as the popcorn boxes–be sure they will not overlap when the card is folded.

1. Transfer the pop-up pattern onto ivory cardstock. Glue wide stripe paper to the cardstock, then the swirl vellum on top. Cut out the pop-up piece. Fold on the dashed lines and crease well. Put tacky tape on the under side of the two narrow flaps–leave the protective strips on.

2. Trim the card to 5" square. Open the card so it lays flat with the fold in the middle. Make a pencil mark on the fold 2" from the top. Position the pop-up piece face down in the card so that the center fold is aligned with the pencil mark and each end of the pop-up piece is even with the top of the card (see diagram). Glue the flaps to the card. Close the card and trim off the excess corners so that they line up with the angle of the pop-up edge.

3. Cut two 5"x⁵⁄₁₆" wide strips of blue vellum with one straight edge and the other with the cloud scissors. Glue the strips along the base of the pop-up. Cut one extra cloud "bump" for the center of the base.

4. Cut out a star from blue vellum and glue as shown. Glue the bowl onto the star.

5. Use the pattern to cut out two pieces of red foam and one piece of white foam for the popcorn box. Glue together with white in the middle. Cut two ¹⁄₁₆" wide strips of white foam and glue to the box. Repeat for the second box. Attach to the pop-up. Glue beads on the top of the popcorn boxes, along the edge and in the bowl as shown.

6. Use foam tape to attach the "Party!" sign to the gold paper and trim leaving a ⅛" border. Cut the sign in half and attach the pieces with pop dots to the center of the pop-up with half of the sign above the top edge using foam tape. Be sure the pieces are straight and close together so when the card is open it looks like one piece.

7. Glue two blue and one red rhinestone to either side of the pop-up as shown. Glue on the beer mug and the beer cans.

8. For the ticket: Cut a ¾"x1½" piece of ivory cardstock. With the ¼" hole punch make a half circle in each end. Attach to gold paper leaving a ¹⁄₁₆" border and punch the ends. Use the sticker letters for "movie" and use a black pen to add the details. Glue to the card.

9. Add the message/invitation with the sticker letters. Let the glue dry completely before folding.

Kitchen Shower
by Donna Smith

4"x5¼" white card
cooking pack
¾" wide pink cloth flowers pack
⅞" wide pink organza ribbon pack
pink gingham paper
scallop decorative scissors
⅛" wide hole punch

1 Trim the card on three sides with scallop scissors through both layers.

2 Cut a 1½"x5" piece of pink gingham paper and glue it to the front of the card near the fold. Cut two 4"x5" pieces of pink gingham paper and glue one to the inside front and the other to the inside.

3 With the card closed, fold the two bottom corners upwards to meet at the center of the card to make the "pocket." Punch one hole in each corner, thread ribbon through the holes and tie in a shoestring bow. Glue the apron and accessories as shown.

Baptism
by LeNae Gerig

5"x6½" white card
baptism dress & cross pack
gold paper (from the book Paper Pizazz™ Metallic Gold)
dot vellum (from the book Paper Pizazz™ Vellum Papers, also by the sheet)
fine point black pen
foam adhesive tape

1 Cut a 4¼"x5⅛" vellum rectangle and mat on gold leaving a ¼" border. Glue it to the card front as shown.

2 Cut a 2¼"x2⅝" gold rectangle and attach the dress in the center. Attach it to the card with foam tape. Attach the cross centered below the dress as shown. Use the black pen to write "Baptism" below the cross.

Baptism

Skating Invitation
by Jeanne Jacobowski

5"x7⅛" white card, trimmed to 3⅞"x5¾"
ice skating pack
solid papers: white, powder blue
blue vellum
sticker letters: white, blue
decorative scissors: deckle, scallop
silver pen

1 Cut a 3¾"x5¾" piece of powder blue paper with scallop scissors and glue to the card front.

2 Tear a piece of white paper to 3½"x4¼" and glue to the powder blue paper.

3 With deckle scissors cut two pieces of blue vellum slightly smaller than the torn white piece. Glue to the white paper.

4 Glue the skating dress, skates and medal onto the card.

5 Attach the blue sticker letters to say "You're Invited" and then layer the white letters on top as shown.

6 Use the pen to draw the details as shown.

Celebrate Like Crazy! by Jeanne Jacobowski

5"x7⅛" gold card
black & gold shoe pack
solid papers: black, gold
red swirl patterned paper
eight ³/₁₆" black eyelets
foam adhesive tape
black pen

1 Open the card and insert one black eyelet in each corner of the card front.

2 Cut a 2" square of gold and mat on black leaving a ¼" border. Insert one eyelet in each corner of the gold. Glue the shoe centered on the gold. Cut a 3½" square of red swirl paper and attach with foam tape centered on the card front. Glue the shoe and papers centered on the red swirl.

3 Add the message with the black pen.

*P*lush velvet hearts, realistic fabric flowers, pretty papers and vellums all work together to provide the perfect romantic feelings in handmade cards. Additional details, such as "Love" formed from wire, brings a personal touch to greetings. Consider using the ideas included in this section to add romance to your special cards.

*T*he distinctive embellishments from The Card Connection help you create a unique card, conveying your own feelings. Adorned with elegant sheer ribbons or shiny metallic cords, and you have a greeting that will become a keepsake. Whether playful or pretty, a handmade romantic card tells the recipient just how cherished they are—and with these embellishments, it's easy to do!

Window to the Heart

by Kelly Woodard

5"x7⅛" purple card
embossed heart seals pack
heart shaped message pack
vellum: white roses, white iridescent fleck
gold pen
X-acto® knife, ruler, cutting surface, pencil

1. Trim the card to a 5" square. Glue a 5" square piece of flecked vellum to the card front. Draw a square in the center of the card front, ¾" in from each side. Use the knife to cut out the square from the card front.

2. Cut a 4¾" square of roses vellum and glue to the inside of the window. Place one heart seal in each corner.

3. On the card front attach one heart seal to each corner covering the first seals.

4. Take the cut out square from Step 2 and attach it as a diamond to the inside of the card. Glue the heart shaped message to it and outline the diamond with the gold pen.

inside

Champagne

by Jeanne Jacobowski

5"x7⅛" white card
champagne glasses pack
solid papers: white, silver
silver writing on vellum
white handmade paper with metallic flecks

12" of ¹¹/₁₆" wide silver screen ribbon
clear micro beads
two ³/₁₆" silver eyelets
deckle decorative scissors

1. Cut the vellum to 5"x7⅛". Be sure the writing is straight. Trim both short sides and one long side with the deckle scissors.

2. Open the card and lay flat. Insert eyelets ⅛" from the fold and 2" from the top and bottom through the vellum and the card front. Thread the ribbon through the eyelets and knot on the front of the card. Trim the ends at an angle.

3. Cut a 1⅝"x1¾" piece of handmade paper and mat on silver leaving a ⅛" border. Mat again on white leaving a ¹/₁₆" border. Glue to the card front as shown.

4. Glue the champagne glasses as shown. Add glue to the tops of the glasses and sprinkle with the beads. Shake off excess and repeat until all of the gaps are filled.

Love and Roses

by Donna Smith

5¼" square white card
red rose bouquet pack
red wire "Love" pack
solid papers: black, gold, white with metallic
flecks, red

1 Cut a 5" square of black and glue centered on the card front. Cut a 4³/₁₆" square of red and glue centered on the black. Cut a 4" square of gold and glue centered on the red. Cut a 3⅝" square of flecked paper and glue centered on the gold.

2 Cut two 1" squares of black then cut diagonally making four triangles. Glue one to each corner of the flecked as shown.

3 Glue the bouquet and wire "Love" to the flecked paper.

For My Love by Susan Cobb

5"x7⅛" gold card
velvet heart pack
patterned paper: burgundy/gold roses, burgundy/gold
checks, solid gold (from the book Paper Pizazz™ Metallic
Gold)
22" of ⅜" wide sheer ivory ribbon
12" of 24-gauge wire
foam adhesive tape
wire cutters, pliers
black pen
X-acto® knife, cutting surface

1 Cut a 4"x6⅛" piece of burgundy/ gold roses paper and glue centered on the card front. Open the card and use the knife to cut a 2¾" square window in the card front, centered on the roses paper.

2 Cover the inside of the card with gold paper. Cut a 2½" square of burgundy/gold checks paper and glue it to the gold paper centered in the front window. Glue the heart to the center of the square. Cut two 4"x½" strips of gold paper and attach with foam tape to the card front, one above and one below the window.

3 Cut the wire in half and coil the ends with pliers as shown then attach one piece to each gold strip.

4 For the ribbon: Start at the bottom center and glue the end to the gold strip. Wrap the ribbon around the wire, knotting as shown. Cut a 3" length of ribbon, tie in a knot and attach over the ribbon ends. Write the message with the black pen.

Wire Love
by Kelly Woodard

5"x7⅛" maroon card
silver wire "Love" pack
vellum: white, white hearts & dots, heart flowers
paper: dark red, pastel pink stripe, white floral,
   embossed white stripe
deckle decorative scissors
foam adhesive tape
E-6000®

1 Trim the card to 5" square. Cut the following
  papers with the deckle scissors:
• white hearts & dots vellum: 5" square
• pink stripe: 4½" square
• white floral: 4" square
• white stripe embossed: 3" square
• heart flowers on vellum: 2½" square

2 Cut a 1¾" square of red paper. Tear a 1¾" square
  of white vellum and glue to red paper. Glue the
wire "Love" with E-6000® and set aside to dry.

3 Glue the pieces to the card starting with the largest
  as shown. Use foam tape to attach the "Love"
square to the card.

Especially for You
by Gina Smith

5"x7⅛" white card
envelope, rose & tag pack
paper: white, pink stripe
gold cord
southwest decorative corner punch

1 Cut the pink stripe paper to
  4¾"x6⅞" with the stripes
vertical. Punch the corners
and glue centered on the card
leaving the corners loose.

2 Cut 4' of the gold cord.
  Leaving 8" loose, start
at the top left corner and
wrap around each corner and
notches. Tie the ends in a
shoestring bow.

3 Cut a 3" square of white
  paper and punch the

corners. Glue to the card as
shown leaving the corners
loose.

4 Cut 30" of gold cord.
  Glue one end of the cord
to the back of the white paper
and wrap around each corner.
Trim the ends and glue to the
back.

5 Glue the rose to the center
  of the white square.

Heart Charm
by Jeanne Jacobowski

5¼" square white card
gold charms pack
paper: magenta, white handmade, white wispy
  mulberry
vellum: white hearts & dots, white
magenta embroidery floss, needle
deckle decorative scissors

3 Tear a piece of handmade paper slightly smaller than the vellum and glue to the card.

4 Trace the envelope pattern onto the heart vellum with a pencil. Cut out so no pencil marks show and fold on the dashed lines into the envelope. Glue where the points overlap and press the edges down.

5 Tear a piece of magenta paper slightly larger than the envelope and glue the envelope to it.

6 Put a 1½" square of torn mulberry paper in the envelope.

7 Thread the needle with floss and insert from the back of the card flap. Slip on the charm and reinsert as shown. Glue the floss behind the flap and tie a knot just above the charm.

1 Cut a 5¼"x10½" of magenta paper the same size as the card. Fold in half and glue to the outside of the card. Trim the front short edge with deckle scissors.

2 Tear a piece of white vellum into an irregular shape a little smaller than the card front. Glue it to the card.

Love Tag
by Donna Smith

5"x7⅛" pink card   *pink decorating chalk*
round silver tag pack   *solid papers: pink,*
sheer ribbon pack   *fuchsia, white, silver*
pink heart rhinestones   *foam adhesive tape*
  pack

1 Trim the card to 5" square. Cut a 5¾" square of fuchsia and glue on the back of the card.

2 Cut a 3½" square of silver and glue centered on the card front. Cut a 3¼" square of fuchsia and glue centered on the silver square. Cut a 1⅝"x3¼" piece of pink and glue on the right side of the fuchsia square.

3 Cut a 3" square piece of pink and glue centered on top. Cut a 1½"x3" piece of fuchsia and attach to the right side of the pink square.

4 Journal "Love" on white paper, then chalk it. Glue it centered on the tag. Cut a 5" length of sheer pink ribbon and thread it through the tag as shown. Attach the tag to the card with foam tape. Attach a rhinestone in each corner and to the tag as shown.

Vellum with Rose Bouquet

4"x5¼" vellum card
white ribbon rose bouquet pack
silver paper
four ³⁄₁₆" white eyelets
1 yard of white coated wire

1. Cut two 3" squares of silver paper. Glue one centered on the card front.

2. Open the card and insert one eyelet just outside each corner of the silver square.

3. Cut the wire into four equal lengths. Put one length on each side of the square with the ends through the eyelets to the inside of the card. From the inside, pull the wire ends together and loosely loop them over each other.

4. Glue the remaining silver square to the inside front exactly behind the other square. Press on firmly.

5. Glue the bouquet centered on the card front.

Love

by Kelly Woodard

5"x7⅛" white card
white daisy pack
solid papers: white, pink
patterned paper: pink gingham, pink glitter embossed
optional: Sizzix machine and letter die-cuts

1. Cut a 4½"x6¾" piece of gingham paper and glue to the card front. Cut a 3"x4" piece of white and glue to the gingham paper.

2. Cut the letters from pink glitter paper using the patterns or the die-cuts. Glue them to the white paper.

3. Cut a 1½"x2" piece of pink paper and glue to white paper as shown.

4. Glue the flower to pink paper.

Valentine
by Jackie Jernstrom

one 5¼" square white card
red sequin confetti hearts pack
solid papers: red, white
cloudy white vellum

1 Cut a 5" square of red and glue it centered on the card front.

2 Cut a 4¾" square of cloudy white vellum and glue it centered on the red.

3 Cut a 4¾" square of white. Use the pattern on page 80 to cut out the windows and glue it on top of the white vellum.

4 Glue the hearts to the white squares as shown.

He Loves Me!

by Jeanne Jacobowski

5"x6½" white card
butterflies pack
1" wide daisies pack
blue vellum (from the book Paper Pizazz™ 12"x12" Pastel Vellum Papers, also by the sheet)
white paper

patterned papers: yellow check, blue swirls, green dot, green plaid (from the book Paper Pizazz™ Bright Tints)
1" leaf punch
optional: large wave decorative scissors
black pen

1 Cover the card front with yellow check paper.

2 Cut a 4½"x6" piece of blue swirls paper and mat it on white with a ¹⁄₁₆" border. Glue it centered on the card front. Cut a 4½"x6" piece of blue vellum and trim it with the wave scissors so it is 4"x5½". Glue it centered on the blue swirls paper.

3 Punch out five green dot and five green plaid leaves. Glue them to the card as shown.

4 Attach seven paper daisies and four butterflies to the card as shown.

5 Use the black pen to add the message and the penwork dashes to the vellum.

Friends Forever

5"x6½" white card
daisy heart with "Friends Forever" pack
blue cording
patterned papers: blue gingham, yellow dots (from the book Paper Pizazz™ Soft Tints)
white paper

1 Trim the card so it is 4½" wide. Cut a 4¼"x6¼" piece of gingham paper and glue it centered on the card front.

2 Cut a 3⅛"x5⅛" piece of dots paper and mat it on white leaving a ⅛" border. Cut three 6½" lengths of cording and wrap them around the dots paper as shown, securing the ends to the back. Glue the dots paper centered on the card front.

3 Glue the heart and plaque to the card as shown.

Love, with Butterfly

by LeNae Gerig

5"x6½" white card
heart from laser cut pack
ribbon and bead butterfly pack
sheer ribbon pack

patterned papers: green swirls, butterflies (from the book Paper Pizazz™ Mixing Soft Papers)

1 Trim the card to 5" square and cover the front with swirls paper. Tear a 1¾" wide strip of butterflies paper and glue it to the bottom of the card front as shown. Trim the edges even with the card.

2 Glue the heart and butterfly to the card front as shown. Cut a 12" length of ¼" wide sheer lavender ribbon. Tie a shoestring bow with ¾" loops and a 1½" tail and a 4" tail. Glue the bow to the card as shown, then glue down the tails. Trim the tails even with the card edges.

What better way to congratulate the bride and groom than with a card you created just for them? Using bridal elements from The Card Connection, gorgeous wedding greetings can be customized for treasured keepsakes.

Decorate a rich metallic blank card with filmy, transparent vellum and a beautiful wedding dress or the satin and pearl cake for an elegantly unique greeting. Or, for the contemporary bride, play with a flower punch and rhinestones to design an invitation like the one featured on page 35.

Not just for cards, many of these elements can also be used to create unique wedding favors and decorations. Embellishments can be added to votive cups, candles, organza bags of mints and small jars of bubbles for perfect, yet inexpensive favors.

There are many options to use in designing unique wedding decorations, cards, engagement cards, thank you notes and place cards; you may find it hard to choose just one! Enjoy the process of combining all the varied elements to create your own personal style.

Pink Rhinestone You're Invited
by Jeanne Jacobowski

two 4"x5¼" cards: one pink, one white
solid papers: white, pink, silver

eight ¼" pink rhinestones
⅝" flower punch
silver sticker letters

1 Trim ³⁄₁₆" off each side of the white card. Glue only the backs of the cards, white on top of the pink.

2 Open the white card front. Make four dots with a pencil ¾" from the edges and 1" apart. Turn the punch upside down and slide onto the card until you can see the dot. Center the pencil dot in the flower opening and punch. Repeat. Glue the card fronts together.

3 Cut a 5⅜"x4⁹⁄₁₆" piece of silver and fold over 2", crease well. Glue over the fold of the cards, with the short side in the front. Punch four flowers out of pink and glue to the top edge of the silver. Glue a rhinestone to the center of each flower.

4 Cut a 12"x1⅛" piece of white. Cut a 12"x1" piece of pink and glue centered on the white. Wrap it around the card in the center and glue overlapping the two ends. Be sure that it is tight enough to stay on, but not so tight that it warps the card.

5 Add the message with the sticker letters.

Heart
by Arlene Peterson

5"x6½" white card
heart pack
cording pack
gold paper (from the book Paper Pizazz™ Metallic Gold)
patterned papers: tan floral, love stamp (from the book Paper Pizazz™ Busy Scrapper's Solution for Wedding & Romance)

1 Cover the card front with gold paper. Cut a 5"x6" piece of floral paper and tear one long edge. Glue it centered on the card front as shown.

2 Cut out the love stamp and mat it on gold leaving a ⅛" border. Glue it and the heart to the card at angles as shown.

3 Tie the cording around the card fold. Trim the tails to 1" and glue in place.

Bridal Shower
by LeNae Gerig

5"x6½" white card
purple paper flowers multi pack
white vellum
purple stripe patterned paper (from the book Paper Pizazz™
    Mixing Soft Patterned Papers)
8" of ⅜" wide sheer white ribbon
lavender eyelets

1 Cut a 4¾"x6⅛" piece of stripe paper and glue it centered on the card front.

2 Journal the message on the vellum and trim it to 2⅞"x4⅝". Attach it to the left side of the card with eyelets as shown.

3 Glue the ribbon to the right side of the card, securing the ends to the inside front. Attach the flowers to the ribbon as shown.

We Are Engaged
by LeNae Gerig

5"x6½" white card
champagne glasses with beads pack
blue hearts rhinestone pack
blue swirls patterned paper (from the book
    Paper Pizazz™ Bright Tints)
solid papers: white, silver
9" of ⅜" wide sheer white ribbon
white vellum
foam adhesive tape

1 Cut a 4½"x6" piece of swirls paper and glue it centered on the card front. Turn the card so the fold is at the top.

2 Cut a 2½"x3" piece of white paper and mat it on silver leaving a ¹⁄₁₆" border. Attach the glasses as shown. Attach the rectangle to the left side of the card with foam tape.

3 Journal "We Are Engaged" on the vellum, leaving room for the bow and heart as shown. Glue it to the right side of the card, then attach the bow and heart.

Best Wishes!

by Jackie Jernstrom

4"x5¼" white card
wedding ring/best wishes pack
papers: white iridescent stripe, gold moiré
foam adhesive tape

1 Cover the card front with gold moiré. Cut a 2¼"x2⅝" piece of stripe paper with the stripes running on the vertical. Glue the ring tied with ribbon. Glue to the front of the card ¾" down from the top and ⅞" in from the sides.

2 Attach the "Best Wishes!" message with foam tape centered beneath the ring.

Will You Be My Bridesmaid?

by Kelly Woodard

5"x7⅛" gold card
ribbon dress & flowers pack
orange/pink sheer ribbon pack
ivory vellum
imperial decorative scissors
ribbon hole punch or X-acto® knife
foam adhesive tape

1 Cut a 4⅞"x7" piece of vellum with the imperial scissors and glue to the card front.

2 Punch two holes, or use the knife to cut them, through the vellum and the card ½" from the top and ¾" from each side. Thread the ribbon through and tie a knot. Glue the dress to the card with the hanger under the ribbon.

3 Glue the flowers to the card. Attach the message at the bottom of the card with foam tape.

Special Day Vellum Tag

by Susan Cobb

5"x7¼" white card
white rose bouquet pack
sheer white ribbon with bead center pack
rectangle tag pack
patterned papers: green stripe, white/green lily of the valley
    (from the book Paper Pizazz™ Soft Florals & Patterns)
white paper
sage green vellum
black pen

1 Cut a 4¾"x7" piece of striped paper and glue it centered on the card front. Measure 2¼" from the bottom right corner of the card front and mark with a pencil. Open the card and cut diagonally from the point you marked to the left top corner. Cover the inside back with lily of the valley paper.

2 Cover a large white tag with sage green vellum. Mat it on white paper leaving a ¹⁄₁₆" border. Write the greeting on the tag with the black pen, then add the border as shown.

3 Glue the tag to the card front as shown. Glue the bow to the top of the tag. Glue the rose bouquet to the lower left corner of the card front.

Wedding Bouquet

by Lisa Garcia-Bergstedt

5"x7⅛" white card
peach and white rose bouquet pack
"Wishing you a lifetime…" sticker message
patterned papers: roses, pink lace, pink moiré (from the book
    Paper Pizazz™ Pretty Papers)
paper: gold (from the book Paper Pizazz™ Metallic Papers)
16" of ⅝" wide sheer white ribbon with white and gold trim

1 Cut a 4¾"x6⅞" piece of rose paper and mat on gold paper leaving a ¹⁄₁₆" border. Glue centered on the card front.

2 Cut a 3⅞"x6" piece of pink moiré paper and mat on gold leaving a ¹⁄₁₆" border. Cut the ribbon into four 4" lengths. Wrap one length around each corner and glue on the back of the gold paper. Glue centered on the rose paper.

3 Cut a 3"x5" piece of lace paper and mat on gold leaving a ¹⁄₁₆" border. Glue centered on the moiré.

4 Glue the bouquet centered on the lace paper and attach the "Wishing you a lifetime of happy days!" sticker message below.

Tuxedo
by Shauna Berglund-Immel

5"x7⅛" silver card
black tuxedo pack
specialty papers: black/silver stripes, silver (from the
book Paper Pizazz™ Metallic Silver Papers)
solid papers: black, white
¹¹/₁₆" wide sheer black ribbon pack
black pen

1 Cut a 4½"x6¾" piece of black/silver stripes and mat on silver leaving a ¹/₁₆" border. Mat on black leaving a ¹/₁₆" border. Glue centered on the card front.

2 Cut a 7"x3½" white strip and mat on black leaving a ¹/₁₆" border. Mat on silver leaving a ¹/₁₆" border. Fold 1" from top and glue the flap to the card back.

3 Glue the tuxedo to the white card flap. Write the message with the black pen. Knot the ribbon and glue as shown.

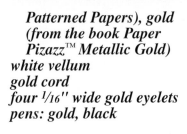

For My Husband On Our Wedding Day

Something Old
by Lisa Garcia-Bergstedt

inside

5"x7⅛" gold card
gold heart locket pack
patterned papers: lace
vellum (from the book
Paper Pizazz™ Vellum
Papers), tan diamonds
(from the book Paper
Pizazz™ Mixing Jewel
Patterned Papers), gold
(from the book Paper
Pizazz™ Metallic Gold)
white vellum
gold cord
four ¹/₁₆" wide gold eyelets
pens: gold, black

1 Cut the card to 5" square. Cut a 4¾" square of diamonds paper and outline the edge with the gold pen. Cut a strip of lace from lace vellum. Wrap the lace vellum on the left side of the square. Glue in the back. Write the messages on white vellum with the black pen. Cut into ½" strips and outline the edges with the gold pen. Glue under the vellum lace and then wrap the right edge under the diamond paper. Glue it centered on the card front.

2 Open the card and attach four gold eyelets along the left edge of the lace and thread the gold cord through. Glue the pendent between the vellum strips, tucking the chain behind the diamonds paper.

3 Cover the inside of the card with gold paper. Cut a 4¾" square of diamond paper and glue centered on the diamond paper. Write the message on white vellum with the black pen and outline gold along the top and bottom. Glue it centered to the inside back.

Wedding Dress

by Jeanne Jacobowski

5³⁄₄"x8³⁄₄" ivory card
wedding dress pack
solid papers: ivory, white
floral embossed white pearl
  vellum
silver gel pen
deckle decorative scissors
¹⁄₈" hole punch

1 Cut a 5"x7³⁄₄" piece of ivory with the deckle scissors and glue centered on the card front.

2 Cut a 4¹⁄₄"x6³⁄₄" piece of white with the deckle scissors and glue centered on the ivory.

3 Cut a 4¹⁄₂"x7¹⁄₄" piece of vellum and glue centered on the white.

4 Write "love • happiness • love • happiness" on the vellum with the silver pen. Let dry completely.

5 Glue the wedding dress centered on the vellum.

Window Wedding Cake

by Jeanne Jacobowski

two 5"x7¹⁄₄" white cards
2 white wedding cake packs
sheer white ribbon flowers
  pack
sheer white ribbon bow
white dot vellum
¹⁄₂" wide sheer white ribbon
scallop decorative scissors
¹⁄₈" hole punch
12" of Stretch Magic™ cord,
  or thread

1 Use the pattern to cut an oval in the front of one card (#1). Place the second card (#2) inside card #1, and lightly trace the oval. Remove and cut the oval out of card #2.

2 Trace a card front and oval lightly onto the vellum. Cut out with straight scissors, then cut three sides with the scallop scissors, leaving the fold side with a straight edge. Cut out the oval ¹⁄₄" smaller from the vellum using the scallop scissors. Erase any pencil marks. Attach the vellum to card #1 with mono adhesive. Glue two ribbon flowers and one bow to the bottom of the oval.

3 Glue the two wedding cakes back to back with a piece of cord in between. Glue a flower at the top of each cake.

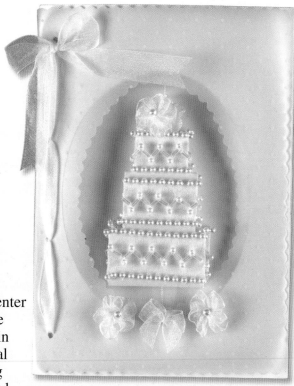

4 Center the cakes in the oval pulling the cord slightly taut, tape to hold. Trim the long edges of card #2 with scallop scissors. Glue card #2 inside card #1.

5 Punch four holes on the front left side of the cards 1¹⁄₂" apart and ¹⁄₄" from the fold. Thread half of the ribbon through the bottom hole and weave the both ends through each hole. Tie a shoestring bow at the top.

Wedding Veil

by Arlene Peterson

5"x6½" white card
tulle veil pack
wire beaded "Love" pack
pink words paper (from the book Paper Pizazz™ Busy
  Scrapper's Solution for Wedding & Romance)
silver paper (from the book Paper Pizazz™ Metallic Silver)
pink cording

1 Cover the card front with silver paper. Cut a 5"x4¾" piece of words paper and glue it centered on the card front.

2 Glue the veil and wire "Love" to the card as shown. Wrap the cord around the fold of the card and knot near the top. Trim the tails to 2½" then unravel them.

Floral Wedding Dress

by Donna Smith

5"x7¼" dark green card
wedding dress with flowers pack
white vellum
gold paper
embossed floral patterned paper

1 Cut gold to 4¾"x7" and glue centered on the card front. Cut embossed floral paper to 4¼"x6½" and glue centered on the gold. Cut vellum to 3¼"x5½" and glue centered on the floral paper.

2 Cut two ½" square pieces of gold and cut diagonally into four triangles. Glue one to each corner of the vellum.

3 Glue the wedding dress centered on the vellum.

*W*hether you're making one very special card for a baby gift or inviting several friends to a baby shower, the whimsical and delicate baby embellishments from The Card Connection will turn cards into keepsakes for baby's album. Bunnies to bears to lambs, these adorable decorations bring warmth and personality to all baby cards, invitations and announcements.

*I*n addition to cards, the photo above shows how versatile these embellishments can be and how well they work together. Sweet fabric appliques, cuddly crocheted pieces and unique charms all blend together, providing a coordinated look to the entire setting. The Card Connection's many baby elements are the perfect finishing touches to all your baby projects, from cards to floral arrangements!

Blue Sweater
by Jeanne Jacobowski

5"x7¼" powder blue card
knitted blue baby sweater pack
solid papers: white, powder blue
white vellum
2½ yards of ¼" wide sheer white ribbon
³⁄₁₆" eyelets: four white, four light blue
foam adhesive tape

1 Cut a 3⅞" square of powder blue paper. Cut a 3⅝" square of vellum and glue centered on the powder blue. Insert a light blue eyelet in each corner. Thread ribbon through the eyelets framing all four sides. Tie the ends in the back.

2 Cut a 4" square of white and attach the powder blue square centered on top with foam tape. Glue the white square centered on the card front.

3 Insert a white eyelet in each corner of the card front. Thread ribbon through the eyelets, framing all four sides. Glue the blue baby sweater centered on the vellum.

Two Babies
by Jackie Jernstrom

5¾"x8¾" white card
babies pack
clear sticker invitation sheet
solid papers: blue, pink, yellow
paper: white, white corrugated
scallop decorative scissors
foam adhesive tape

1 With the fold at the top, trim the short side of the card to 4¾".

2 Cut a 8½"x4½" piece of blue paper and glue centered on the card front. Cut a 8¼"x4¼" piece of pink paper with the scallop scissors and glue centered on the light blue paper. Cut a 8"x4" piece of yellow paper and glue centered on the pink paper. Cut a 7¾"x3¾" piece of white corrugated paper and glue centered on the yellow paper.

3 Cut one 2"x3¼" piece from both pink and blue papers. Glue the pink baby to the blue rectangle and the blue baby to the pink rectangle.

4 Use foam tape to attach the blue baby to the left side of the card, with a ¼" border. Glue the pink baby to the right side of the card in the same manner.

5 Attach the invitation sheet to a piece of white paper and trim with the scallop scissors. Glue it to a 2¼"x2¾" piece of yellow paper then attach to the card with foam tape.

Christening Gown on Vellum
by Jeanne Jacobowski

two 4"x5¼" cards: one
   pink, one vellum
christening gown pack
fine gold cording pack
1 yard of ¼" wide white
   sheer ribbon

white vellum
scallop decorative
   scissors
hole punches: ⅛", ¹⁄₁₆"
stylus

1 Trim all three edges of the vellum card with the scallop scissors and punch a ¹⁄₁₆" hole in each bump. Trim the pink card to 3¾"x4¾" with the scallop scissors. Glue the pink card inside the vellum card.

2 Cut an oval from vellum using the pattern and scallop scissors. Punch a ¹⁄₁₆" hole in each bump. Glue centered on the vellum card front then glue the gown to the center of the oval.

3 Punch two ⅛" holes in the folds of the cards, ½" from the top and bottom. Cut the ribbon in half and thread both pieces together through the holes from the inside. Tie in a shoestring bow at the top as shown. Thread the cross on the gold cord and tie to the bow.

It's A Girl
by Jeanne Jacobowski

5½" square white card
ribbon & baby shoes
   charm pack
sheer ribbon pack
baby stickers pack
vellum: pink, white dot,
   white with flowers

silver paper (from the
   book Paper Pizazz™
   Metallic Silver)
⅛" hole punch

1 Tear a 5"x4" piece of pink vellum and glue to the card leaving room for the sticker at the bottom. Tear a 4¼"x3½" piece of flower vellum and glue centered on the card front. Tear a 3¾"x3" piece of pink vellum and glue centered on the card front. Tear 3½"x2½" piece of white dot vellum and glue centered on the pink vellum.

2 Tear a 2¼" square piece of silver paper. Tear a 1½" square of pink vellum and glue it to the silver paper as shown. Thread the charm on the ribbon and wrap it round the silver paper three times, securing the ends in the back. Glue it centered on the card. Attach the sticker to the bottom of the card front. Punch two holes through the pink vellum and the card front ½" from the top and 2" from each side. Thread the ribbon through the holes from inside the card and tie a bow on the card front as shown.

Pink Buggy

5"x6½" white card
pink buggy pack
"Congratulations on your new daughter!" from vellum
    messages pack
satin bow pack
silver paper (from the book Paper Pizazz™ Metallic Silver)
"It's a Girl" patterned paper (from the book Paper Pizazz™
    Baby's First Year)
pink vellum

1 Cover the card front with pink vellum. Cut a 4⅞"x6¼" piece of "It's a Girl!" paper and glue it centered on the card front.

2 Glue a 3" square of pink vellum centered on the card front. Cut a 2"x2¾" piece of silver paper and glue it centered on the vellum. Attach the buggy to the card as shown.

3 Glue the heart message to a 1¼"x1⅛" piece of silver paper then mat it on vellum leaving a ⅛" border. Glue it centered on a 5"x½" vellum strip, then glue it to the card as shown. Glue a pink bow to the left of the message.

Booties & Bottles Tri-fold
by Donna Smith

two 5" square white cards
crocheted booties pack
pink baby outfit pack
blue baby outfit pack
bottles/carriage pack
pastel sheer ribbons pack
patterned papers: bottles/bunnies, pink tri-dot,
    blue tri-dot (from the book Paper Pizazz™
    Baby's First Year)
black pen

1 Glue the cards together to form the tri-fold card (see diagram). Cover the card front and the two inside panels with bottles/bunnies paper.

2 Glue a pink ribbon to the middle of the front panel of the card so 10¾" is loose on the left side and 5½" is loose on the right side.

3 Cut three 3" squares of blue tri-dot paper and mat each on pink tri-dot paper leaving ⅜" borders. Glue one centered to each panel.

4 Glue the bottles, booties and outfits to the card as shown. Let dry.

5 Close the card, wrap the left end of the ribbon around the back of the card and tie a bow on the right side of the card front. Write the message with the black pen.

unfolded

Little Onesie
by Jeanne Jacobowski

5"x6½" white card
blue onesie pack
duck & bottle pack
solid papers: powder blue, white
blue vellum

1 Tear a 3¼"x4¼" piece of white paper. Tear ¼"-½" wide, uneven strips of powder blue paper. Glue them to the white paper as shown.

2 Repeat with blue vellum.

3 Glue the white paper with the strips to powder blue paper and tear an uneven ¼" border.

4 Glue the white paper with the strips to powder blue paper and tear an uneven ¼" border.

5 Glue the powder blue paper to blue vellum and tear a ⅛" border. Attach the onesie and duck as shown and attach to the card front.

Baby Shower

by Kelly Woodard

5"x7⅛" purple card
crocheted chick pack
"Baby Shower" message
solid papers: lavender, white
white swirl vellum
¼" wide lavender with gold ribbon
majestic decorative scissors
³⁄₁₆" square punch

1 Cut a 4½"x6¾" piece of vellum with the majestic scissors and place on the card front. Punch two holes through the vellum and the card front ½" from the top and 1¾" from each side. Thread the ribbon through and tie a shoestring bow.

2 Use the pattern to cut the egg from lavender paper. Glue the chick to the back of the egg, fold closed and punch square holes following the pattern. Thread ribbon through the holes and tie a bow to hold the egg closed.

3 Cut a 2½"x1" piece of white paper with the majestic scissors. Add the "Baby Shower" message and glue to the vellum as shown.

It's A Boy!

by Lisa Garcia-Bergstedt

5¼" square white card
blue gingham bunny pack
³⁄₁₆" eyelets: four willow green, four royal blue
patterned papers: blue/green plaid, green
  watercolor stripes
white vellum
blue pen
X-acto® knife, cutting surface

1 Open the card face up. Use the knife to cut a 2⅜" square in the center of the card front, set aside. Cut a 5" square of the plaid paper. Use the knife to cut a 2¾" square in the center. Glue the plaid square centered on the card front.

2 Open the card and glue a 5" square of stripes paper centered on the inside back. Cut four 5"x¾" strips of white vellum. Place a strip ⅛" from the top and and another from the bottom edges of the striped square. Insert a blue eyelet at each end. Repeat on the card front with the two remaining vellum strips and green eyelets.

3 Add the messages with the blue pen. Glue the bunny to the inside back, centered in the window.

inside

Boy Angel

by Jeanne Jacobowski

inside

5¼" square white card
boy angel & "Little Angel" pack
solid papers: blue, silver
sticker letters: white, silver
silver gel pen
½" star punch
scallop decorative scissors
foam adhesive tape

1 With the scallop scissors cut a 4¾"x10" piece of blue and fold in half. Use the pattern to cut a circle out of the card front. Put the card inside the blue and lightly trace the circle onto the blue. Remove the card and cut out inside the circle with the scallop scissors. Glue the blue to the card.

2 Glue the angel in the opening. Use the white sticker letters to put "Welcome" above the opening and attach the "Little Angel" sticker below the opening.

3 Punch 10 stars from silver. Use foam tape to attach eight on the front of the card and two on the inside 1" below the angel's hands.

4 With the silver pen draw squiggly lines from the stars to the top of the card. At the top of each line draw a bow. On the inside, draw a bow next to each hand, and a string to each star. Use the silver letters to put "Congratulations!" above the angel on the inside of the card.

Baby Charms

by Donna Smith

5½" square white card
silver baby charms pack
newborn's photograph
vellum: white, baby blue
white paper
1½" wide sheer baby blue ribbon with satin
  edges
cloud decorative scissors
pliers, needle
silver pen

1 Cut a 5½"x11" piece of white vellum and fold in half. Place the card inside the vellum and trim off ½" of the card and vellum on all sides with the cloud scissors.

2 Cut three 1½" squares of white and four 1¾" squares of blue vellum.

3 To attach a charm to each white square, use the wire that is included with the charms. Cut the wire into thirds and shape each piece into a "U." Use the needle to poke two holes in the squares. Put the wire through the ring on the charm and then thread it through the holes. On the back of the white squares press the wires flat like a staple.

4 Glue the white squares to the vellum squares. Attach them to the card as shown. Crop the baby photo to 1½" square and glue to the blank vellum square. Tie a shoestring bow and glue as shown. Use the silver pen to outline the white squares and photo.

Blanket & Pacifier

by Shauna Berglund-Immel

5"x6½" white card
silver baby charms pack
baby blanket pack
baby collage paper pack
sheer ribbon pack

1 Cover the card front with stars paper.

2 Glue the "A Special Delivery" and "Baby Girl" banners as shown. Glue the blanket between the banners. Glue "It's A Girl" heart to the blanket as shown. Tie a thin white ribbon to the pacifier charm and glue it to the blanket.

3 Glue the bunny to the bottom right corner. Tie a shoestring bow with the sheer ribbon and glue as shown.

Pacifier & Bottle
by Donna Smith

3¼"x5¼" white card
baby items pack
pastel cardstock pack
handmade paper pack
pastel cording pack
patterned paper: pink gingham, pink swirls
  (from the book Paper Pizazz™ Soft Tints)
one ⅜" white button

1 Cover the card front with swirls paper. Cut a 4¾"x1½" piece of pink gingham and mat on white paper leaving a narrow border. Glue it to the top of the card, flush with the fold.

2 Stitch cording through the button holes, leaving 2" on each side. Glue the button ¼" from the top of the card and the cording ends to the card as shown.

3 Cut a 4¼"x1¾" piece of white and mat it on yellow with a ¹/₁₆" border. Glue it to card overlapping the cord ends.

4 Tear one 1" square from yellow, pink and green. Glue them to the white as shown. Glue the items as shown.

Bib & Pacifier by Donna Smith

5¼" square white card
pink bib and pacifier pack
solid papers: pink, blue, white
⅛" wide pink satin ribbon
three ⅝" white buttons
cloud decorative scissors

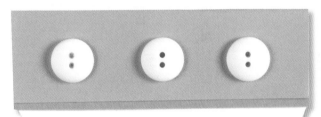

1 With the fold at the top, trim to 4½" wide. Then trim the three open sides with the cloud scissors.

2 Cut a 4"x2¾" piece of blue and fold it in half. Glue to the fold so half of the blue is on the front of the card and half is on the back.

3 Cut a 4"x2½" piece of pink and fold in half. Glue over the blue. Glue on the buttons.

4 On the front of the card, score a line just below the blue and crease well. Open the card and glue the inside front and back to each other above the score line.

5 Cut a 3⅛" square of pink and glue it to the card. Cut a 3" square of white and glue to the pink.

6 Glue the bib and pacifier to the white. Tie a shoestring bow to the pacifier handle.

Connecting with friends is especially important—even when done just for the fun of it! Beaded or wire flowers, a sassy cat, a fuzzy dog, or even a piece of fancy clothing are great embellishments to use in creating your card, depending on the message you're sending. These playful embellishments make your greeting easy to create.

Add sparkling ribbons and cording, shining rhinestones, or even sticker messages to provide the finishing touches. Fun cards are easy to make, exciting to receive and allow you to celebrate all your friendships in a personal and heartwarming way. Enjoy creating your special messages using all the fun embellishments to customize your cards!

Go Team!
by LeNae Gerig

5"x6½" white card
cheerleader pack
clear star rhinestones pack
black/silver striped patterned paper (from the
book Paper Pizazz™ Metallic Silver)
black paper
black pen

1 Cut a 4½"x5¼" piece of striped paper and mat it on black leaving a ¹⁄₁₆" border. Glue it to the card front as shown.

2 Attach the cheerleader costume and banner on the striped paper as shown. Use the black pen to write the message on the bottom of the card. Attach a star on each side.

 Hurray! Great Job!!!

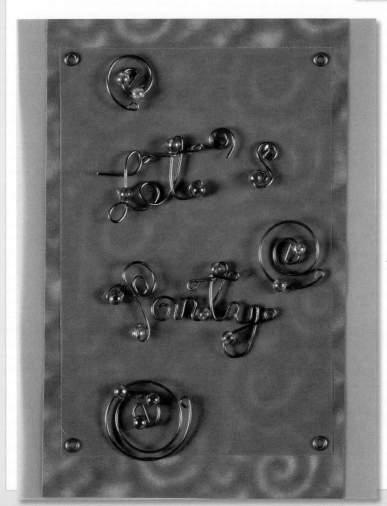

Let's Party
by Arlene Peterson

5"x6½" white card
"Let's Party" wire words pack
wire swirls pack
purple swirl patterned paper (from the book
Paper Pizazz™ Great Backgrounds)
lavender vellum
four ³⁄₁₆" silver eyelets

1 Cover the card front with vellum. Cut a 6½"x4" piece of swirl paper and glue it to the card as shown.

2 Cut a 4"x5¼" piece of vellum and attach it centered on the card front with an eyelet in each corner. Glue on the wire words and swirls as shown.

Little Princess
by Donna Smith

5"x6½" pink card
pink dress/balloons pack
white dots vellum
white paper
pink flowers patterned paper (from the book Paper Pizazz™ Soft Tints, also by the sheet)
four 3/16" white eyelets
scallop decorative scissors

1 Cut a 4½"x6" piece of white dots vellum and attach it to the card front with an eyelet in each corner.

2 Use the pattern to cut an oval out of the pink flowers paper. Mat the oval on white and trim with the scallop scissors. Glue it centered on the card front. Arrange and attach the dress to the card front as shown.

A Garden of Love
by LeNae Gerig

5"x6½" white card
gardening pack
yellow gingham patterned paper (from the book Paper Pizazz™ Soft Tints)
floral vellum (from the book Paper Pizazz™ Floral Vellum Papers)
four 3/16" white eyelets

1 Cover the card front with yellow gingham. Trim the vellum to 4⅝"x6⅛" with the flowers as shown. Attach it to the card with an eyelet in each corner.

2 Attach the "Garden of Love" banner, overalls, hat and spade as shown.

Beaded Flower
by Jackie Jernstrom

5"x7⅛" white card
beaded flowers pack
round pink tag
pink cording
pink satin bow
patterned papers: pink
    flowers on yellow,
    pink/yellow gingham
    (from the book Paper
    Pizazz™ Soft Tints)

pastel pink vellum (from
    the book Paper Pizazz™
    12"x12" Pastel Vellum
    Papers)
solid yellow paper
black pen
foam adhesive tape

1 Cover the card front with yellow paper. Cut a 4⅝"x7" piece of floral paper and glue it centered on the card front. Cut a 3"x4" piece of pink vellum and a 3"x4" piece of gingham paper. Glue them to the card front as shown.

2 Glue two beaded flowers to the gingham paper. Glue one end of the pink cording at the side of the bottom flower. Wrap it around the top flower as shown, then glue the end at the other side of the bottom flower.

3 Use the pen to write "Mom" on the tag. Hang it from the bow with cording as shown, then glue them in place.

Luau Invitation by Susan Cobb

5"x6½" white card
luau grass skirt & lei pack
pink tag
purple flower rhinestones
green/white swirls handmade paper
solid purple paper (from the book Paper Pizazz™ Solid
    Jewel Tones)
foam adhesive tape
black pen

1 Cover the card front with swirls paper. Cut a 4½"x5½" piece of purple paper and glue it centered on the card front.

2 Attach the grass skirt, lei, flip flops and menu on the card front as shown.

3 Write "You're Invited!" on the tag with the black pen. Attach the tag to the lower left corner with a rhinestone flower. Add the remaining rhinestones to the corners of the purple paper. Use the black pen to outline the tag and purple paper as shown.

Black & White Dog
by Kelly Woodard

5"x7⅛" red card
crocheted black & white dog pack
yellow paper
paw print patterned paper
⅝" wide red satin ribbon
cloud decorative scissors

1 Cut a 4½"x6½" piece of paw print paper and glue centered on the card front.

2 Cut a 2½"x4½" piece of yellow paper and trim the short edges with the cloud scissors. Glue centered on the paw paper.

3 Glue the dog near the bottom of the yellow paper. Tie a bow with the ribbon and glue above the dog.

Black Cat
by Jeanne Jacobowski

5"x7⅛" white card
black cat and rhinestone swirl pack
black moiré patterned paper
solid papers: white, red
cloud decorative scissors

1 Cut a 4½"x6⅝" piece of black moiré and glue centered on the card front.

2 Cut the small oval out of white paper. Cut the large oval out of red using cloud scissors on the outside edge. Glue the red oval to the card with the white in its center.

3 Glue the cat centered on the card with the blue swirl as shown.

Beach Chairs
by Kelly Woodard

5"x7⅛" white card
beach chairs pack
"Have a Wonderful Trip" message pack
papers: sunset, tan, green
brown tissue paper
micro beads: silver, clear
foam adhesive tape
tacky craft glue

© Sizzix die-cut #38-0183

1 Glue the sunset paper covering the card front. Cut a curved beach shape out of tan paper and glue to the bottom of the card. Cover the tan paper with tacky glue and sprinkle on the micro beads. Shake off the excess beads and let dry.

2 Use the patterns to cut out the palm leaves and trunk from tan paper, the palm leaves from green paper and a coconut from brown tissue paper. Glue the palm leaves and trunk to the card, then attach the leaves and coconut with foam tape. Glue the chairs to the beach and add the message.

Clothesline
by Jackie Jernstrom

5"x7⅛" turquoise card
clothesline pack
yellow flower embossed paper
white woven vellum
solid papers: turquoise, bright yellow, red,
  fuchsia
gold metallic embroidery floss
punches: ⅛" hole, ½" flower
scallop decorative scissors
foam adhesive tape
X-acto® knife, cutting surface

1 Cut a piece of yellow embossed paper the same size as the card front. Trim one of the long edges with scallop scissors. Glue to the card.

2 Cut one 6"x2" piece of vellum and two of turquoise. On one turquoise piece, mark a ¼" border from each edge and cut out a window. Glue the vellum to the turquoise then the frame on top. Glue to the card ⅝" from the top and each side using foam tape.

3 Glue the clothesline pieces so they look like one strand.

4 Cut a 10" piece of floss and fold in half. Tie a bow and glue it to the left end of the clothesline. Cut a 22" piece of floss and fold in half. Tie a bow and glue it to the right end of the clothesline. Trim the two left ends to 2¾", and the two right ends to 4".

5 Punch two red flowers and two fuchsia flowers. Glue the two left ends of floss between the two fuchsia flowers and attach to the card with foam tape. Repeat for the red flowers using the two right ends of floss. Punch two ⅛" circles from yellow and glue to the flower centers.

Friends
by LeNae Gerig

5"x6½" white card
flower & sequin pack
yellow geometric patterned paper (from the book
   Paper Pizazz™ A Girl's Scrapbook)
solid papers: white, blue
18" of ¼" wide dark pink satin ribbon
fine point black pen
foam adhesive tape

1 Cut a 4⅝"x6" piece of geometric paper. Cut the ribbon into four 4½" lengths. Knot the ends together, then glue them to the geometric paper, securing the ends to the back. Trim the tails to ½" long. Glue the paper centered on the card front.

2 Cut a 1⅞" white square and mat it on blue leaving a ¹⁄₁₆" border. Attach the flower to the center, then use the pen to write "friends" around the edges as shown. Attach the square on point to the card front with foam tape.

Hats & Gloves
by Susan Cobb

5"x6½" white card
hats pack
gloves pack
paper tags/ribbons pack
solid burgundy paper
patterned papers: green/pink grid, pink floral (from
   the book Paper Pizazz™ Joy's Vintage Papers)
white pen

1 Cover the card front with grid paper. Tear the top and bottom edges of a 5"x6½" piece of floral paper so it becomes 5"x5½". Glue it centered on the card front, then trim the edges even with the card.

2 Cut a 5"x1½" strip of grid paper and mat it on burgundy leaving a very thin border. Glue it centered on the card front.

3 Attach the hats and gloves to the card as shown. Use the white pen to write "For You" and a dash-dot border on a round pink tag. Use pink satin ribbon to hang the tag from the hat.

Born to Shop
by Susan Cobb

5"x6½" white card
born to shop pack
square green rhinestones
pack
white paper tag pack
handmade paper pack

green watercolor
patterned paper
(from the book
Paper Pizazz™ Great
Backgrounds)
solid white paper

1 Trim the card to 5" square. Cover the card front with watercolor paper.

2 Cut a 4"x3½" piece of yellow handmade paper and glue it centered on the card front. Cut a 2½" square of green handmade paper. Glue it centered on the yellow paper as shown.

3 Glue the born to shop pieces to the card front as shown. Cover the white tag with green handmade paper then mat on white leaving a very thin border. Glue the tag to the card as shown.

4 Use the black pen to write a message on the tag. Add the rhinestones to the card as shown.

Garden Friends
by Susan Cobb

5"x7⅛" white card
flower pot/watering can pack
wire words pack
patterned papers: blue swirls, multi-colored check paper
(from the book Paper Pizazz™ A Girl's Scrapbook)
black paper

1 Cover the card front with check paper. Cut a 4"x3" piece of swirls paper and mat it on black leaving a ¹⁄₁₆" border. Glue it centered on the card front.

2 Separate the flowers and add them to the flower pot. Attach them to the left side of the swirls paper. Attach the watering can to the right side. Attach the grass strip over the top of both.

3 Glue the wire "friend" to the card as shown.

Daughter
by Arlene Peterson

5"x6½" white card
rhinestone butterflies pack
flowers and hearts trim pack
daughter magnet pack
solid mauve paper
patterned papers: blue/purple texture,
*   blue/purple tiles (from the book Paper*
*   Pizazz™ Bright Great Backgrounds)*

1 Cover the card with mauve paper. Cut a 6"x4½" piece of texture paper and glue it centered on the card front. Cut a 2¾"x4" piece of tiles paper and mat it on mauve leaving a ⅛" border. With the card fold at the top, glue it to the left side of the card. Glue the magnet and three butterflies as shown.

2 Cut two 1¾" squares of tile paper and two 2" squares of mauve paper. Layer and glue them to the right side of the card as shown. Attach the flowers and rhinestones to each square as shown.

Gingham Cats
by Jeanne Jacobowski

two 5¾"x8¾" cards: 1 turquoise,
*   1 lime green*
gingham cats pack
solid papers: purple, lime green,
*   fuchsia, corrugated yellow*
³/₁₆" eyelets: 3 yellow, 8 lime green
decorative scissors: cloud, stamp
⅝" flower punch
foam adhesive tape

1 Trim the turquoise card to 4⅜"x8¾". Glue the lime green card inside and trim the long edge with the cloud scissors.

2 Tear a 2¼" square of fuchsia and attach the purple cat with foam tape to the center. Mat on lime green and trim with the stamp scissors leaving a ⅛" border.

3 Repeat attaching the pink cat to a torn square of purple and matting on lime green. Mat on fuchsia leaving a ⅛" border.

4 Attach each to corrugated yellow with foam tape and trim leaving a ¼" border. Center the two squares on the card front as shown and attach to the card with one lime green eyelet in each corner.

5 Punch one flower from purple and one from fuchsia. Use the green gingham flower from the cat pack and insert a yellow eyelet in the center of all three flowers. Attach them to the card with foam tape. Add the message with the black pen.

Red Rose Dress
by Jeanne Jacobowski

6¼" square white card
red paper flower heads pack
silver wire hanger pack
silver rhinestone chain pack
paper: silver, white handmade with metallic
   flecks, dark gold, red
foam adhesive tape

1 Cut a 6" square of dark gold paper and glue centered on the card front. Tear a 5¾" square of silver paper and glue centered on the card. Cut a 5½" square of red and glue centered on top. Tear a 5¼" square of handmade paper and glue centered on the card.

2 Glue the flowers to the handmade paper in the shape of a skirt. Use the pattern to cut the dress top out of silver paper then attach it with foam tape. Glue the hanger behind the dress top.

3 Cut pieces of the rhinestone strand to fit the neck, sleeves and waistband and glue as shown.

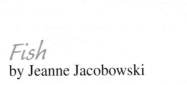

Fish
by Jeanne Jacobowski

5"x6½" white card
sparkle fish pack
bubbles patterned paper (from the book Paper
   Pizazz™ Baby, also by the sheet)
solid papers: aqua, lavender
black pen

1 Cut two 4¼"x6⅞" pieces of bubble paper. Mat each on aqua paper leaving a ¹⁄₁₆" border on each. Glue one to each side of the inside of the card.

2 With the card closed fold the right edge of the front cover back towards the fold, making a Z-fold card.

3 Cut a 2¼" square of bubble paper and double-mat it on aqua and lavender papers leaving a ¹⁄₁₆" border of each. Turn it on point and glue it to the card front as shown. Be sure and glue only the left half of the square to the card font and nothing to the inside back of the card.

4 Attach the fish and bubbles to the card as shown. Use the pen to add the penwork and write a message on the card.

Friendship Connections

Staying connected with friends and family is especially rewarding when making and giving your own cards. It can be simple or elaborate, elegant or whimsical, sentimental or fun. No matter the style you choose, your card will delight the recipient and let them know you cherish their friendship.

The embellishments available are varied and numerous, allowing you to create a unique, one-of-a-kind card every time. Begin by placing different types of papers onto a blank card for a terrific base. There are colorful, textured handmade papers to choose from, along with elegant vellums and lovely patterned papers.

The mood and message you wish to convey will determine which papers and embellishments work together on your card. For example, the gold paper and tassels give the card above a sophistication that the handmade paper embellishement couldn't achieve on its own. Similarly, the layered vellum on the Three Vases card reinforces the contemporary, fresh feeling of the flowers and vases.

Let the backgrounds and embellishments work together to bring your feelings and message of friendship to your card. The choices and combinations of paper styles and dimensional embellishments are nearly endless, giving you the opportunity to create a customized greeting for each friend!

Letter Collage

by Arlene Peterson

5"x6½" white card
letter pack
gold tassel pack
gold cording pack
handmade paper pack
metallic gold paper (from the book Paper
    Pizazz™ Metallic Gold)
green leaf paper (from the book Paper
    Pizazz™ Flowered "Handmade" Papers
    & Vellum)

1 Cover the card front with gold paper. Cut a 5"x4¾" piece of green leaf paper and glue it centered on the card front.

2 Glue the letter, envelope and bouquet centered on green handmade paper as shown, then tear each side so it is 3"x4½". Cut a 3¼"x4⅝" piece of gold and glue it and the handmade paper to the card as shown.

3 Wrap the gold cording around the card front as shown and glue in place. Tie the two tassels together, then glue them to the card.

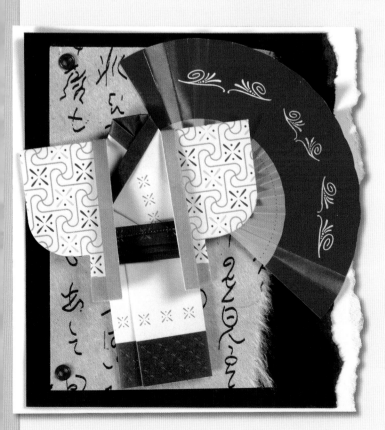

Kimono and Fan

by LeNae Gerig

5"x6½" white card
origami kimono pack
paper fans pack
Asian paper pack
solid black paper
red eyelets

1 Turn the card so the fold is on the left. Tear 2" from the right edge of the card as shown. Cut a 4½" square of black paper and tear one edge as shown.

2 Cut a 4¼"x3" piece of Asian paper. Tear ½" from one long edge. Glue it to the card front as shown.

3 Attach an eyelet in the left corners of the Asian papers as shown. Glue the black paper to the card front centered within the straight edges of the card.

4 Glue the fan and the kimono to the card as shown.

Please write soon!

Letters
by Jeanne Jacobowski

**5"x7⅛" ivory card
letters and charm pack
pink vellum
handmade paper: white with
   gold & silver flecks
ivory cardstock
gold gel pen
deckle decorative scissors**

1 Tear the handmade paper into a rectangle roughly the same size as the letters and glue the letters to it.

2 Tear two rectangles of pink vellum ½" larger than the white paper. Giue behind the handmade paper being sure to hide the glue.

3 Tear another rectangle of handmade paper slightly larger than the pink vellum and glue to the back of the stack.

4 Tear a rectangle of gold slightly larger than the last piece of handmade paper and glue to the back of the stack. Then glue the stack to the card front.

5 Draw a fine gold line around the edge of the card ¼" from the edge. The line should be a very loose, slightly squiggly line.

6 Cut a 2¼"x½" piece of ivory cardstock with the deckle scissors and write the message with the gold pen. Glue to the bottom right corner of the card.

Topiary
by Jeanne Jacobowski

**5"x7⅛" evergreen card
pink sheer ribbon flowers pack
paper flower pots pack
paper: gold, dark green,
handmade: white with metallic
   flecks
ribbons: ⅝" wide pink sheer,
   ¼" pink/gold sheer
tiny dried pressed flowers
sand Twistel™
gold gel pen
deckle decorative scissors
foam adhesive tape**

1 Trim ⅛" off of the card front right edge with the deckle scissors. Cut a 5"x7⅛" piece of gold paper and glue it to the inside front of the card so a border of gold shows behind the deckle edge.

2 Tear a 2¾"x5" piece of gold vellum and glue it to the card front. Tear a 2¼"x5" piece of handmade paper and glue to the gold vellum. Attach the flower pot with foam tape as shown.

*Friends are like flowers...
each one is unique and special.*

3 Cut three 2½" lengths of Twistel™ and twist together then glue the ends. Glue to the card with one end ½" in the pot and the other end straight up.

4 Cut a 4" length of ¼" ribbon and wrap it around the stem several times then glue the end. Trim the ends. With foam tape place the pot front on top of the pot back. Cut a 4" length of pink sheer ribbon and knot it around the stem above the pot. Trim the ends at an angle.

5 With the deckle scissors, cut three 1" circles from green paper. Attach with foam tape to the top of the stem. Glue on the pink roses to the circles then fill in the empty spaces with the dried flowers. Draw a line on the top edge of the pot and write the message with the gold pen.

Thank You

by Lisa Garcia-Bergstedt

5¼" square white card
pressed red flower
pansy patterned paper
vellum: lavender, silver script
12 lime green seed beads
silver pen
ivory thread, needle
foam adhesive tape

1 Measure and center a 4¾" square on the card front. Cut out and set aside. Cut a 5¼" square of script vellum and glue to the inside of the card front. Cut a 3" square from the center of the script vellum.

2 Cut a 5⅛" square of pansy paper and glue centered on the inside back of the card.

3 Cut a 2½" square from the 5" square in Step 1. Mat on lavender vellum with a ¹⁄₁₆" border. Sew three beads to each corner. With the silver pen add the message and outline the squares on the card front. Glue the flower in the white center. Attach with foam tape to the inside of the card.

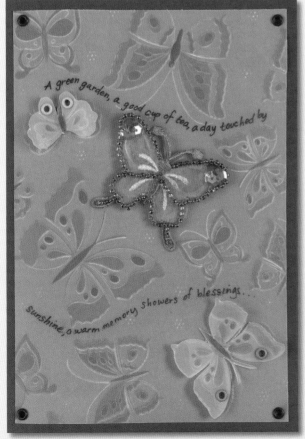

Butterflies

by Lisa Garcia-Bergstedt

5"x7¼" lavender card
beaded lavender butterfly pack
butterfly embossed vellum
³⁄₁₆" eyelets: 4 grape, 2 lemon, 2 willow green
black pen

1 Cut a 4¾"x6⅞" rectangle of butterfly embossed vellum. Attach it centered on the card front by inserting a lavender eyelet in each corner.

2 From the remaining vellum, cut out two butterflies. Insert a willow green eyelet on each upper wing of the larger butterfly and a lemon eyelet on each upper wing of the smaller butterfly. Glue each butterfly body to the vellum as shown, then gently bend the wings upward.

3 Glue the beaded butterfly to the card front as shown. Use the black pen to write the message.

Red Purse
by Jeanne Jacobowski

6½" square white card
red purse pack
"Friends know all…" sticker message pack
gold dots patterned paper (from the book Paper Pizazz™ Metallic Gold)
solid papers: red, black
4 black eyelets
foam adhesive tape

1 Trim the card to 6" square. Cover the card front with red. Cut a 5¾" square of dots paper and mat on black leaving a ¹⁄₃₂" border. Glue centered on the card front.

2 Cut a 2½" square of dots and mat on black leaving a ¹⁄₃₂" border. Mat on red leaving a ¹⁄₃₂" border. Insert one eyelet into each corner. Glue the purse to the center, then attach centered on the card front with foam tape.

3 Attach the sticker message centered below the purse.

Three Vases
by Arlene Peterson

5"x6½" white card
sequined flowers in vases pack
bows pack
paper: words, pink vellum, lavender vellum (from the book Paper Pizazz™ Busy Scrapper's Solution for Wedding & Romance)

1 Cover the card front with words paper.

2 Cut a 5½"x4" piece of each pink and lavender vellum. Glue them to the card as shown.

3 Cut a 4¾"x2¾" piece of words paper and glue it centered on the card. Attach the vases evenly spaced on the words paper, then glue the bow to the vellum as shown.

Down by the Sea
by Shauna Berglund-Immel

5"x6½" white card
bikini, towel, flip flops pack
purple paper
clouds patterned paper (from the book Paper Pizazz™
*   Vacation, also by the sheet)*
scallop decorative scissors
foam adhesive tape
black pen

1 Trim the open edges of the card with the scallop scissors. Cut a 4½"x6" piece of cloud paper and mat it on purple paper leaving a narrow border. Glue it centered on the card front.

2 Glue the towel, bikini and flip flops to the card as shown. Write a message with the black pen.

Houses
by Jackie Jernstrom

5"x7⅛" white card
paper houses pack
solid papers: green, lilac, bright pink,
*   yellow, white, pale pink*
lime green sticker letters
foam adhesive tape

1 Cut a 4½"x5½" piece of pale pink and glue centered on the card front.

2 Cut one 1¾"x2⅛" rectangle from green, yellow, lilac and bright pink. Glue the houses as shown. Attach the two flowers to the green house using foam tape. Set aside.

3 Cut out four 2"x2½" rectangles from white and glue to the pink as shown. Attach one house/rectangle to each white rectangle using foam tape.

4 Cut a 4½"x1" piece of pale pink and glue centered below the houses. Cut a 4¼"x¾" piece of white and glue centered on the pale pink rectangle. Add your message with the sticker letters.

Hi Friend!
by Shauna Berglund-Immel

5"x6½" white card
sheet of dried pressed flowers pack
collage paper pack
primary color ribbons & tags multi pack
solid papers: white, green
black pen

1 Cover the card front with speckled collage paper. Attach the pressed flowers sheet to white paper and trim the white paper leaving a ¹⁄₁₆" border. Mat it on green paper leaving a narrow border.

2 Wrap a yellow ribbon around the flowers and tie a bow as shown. Glue it centered on the card front.

3 Write a message on the tag with the black pen then glue it tucked under the ribbon.

Three Rosebuds
by Jeanne Jacobowski

5¹⁄₄" square ivory card
3 dried rosebuds on paper pack
solid papers: black, gold, gold/black metallic
gold/tan floral patterned paper
deckle decorative scissors

1 Cut a 5" square of gold paper and trim with the deckle scissors on all four sides. Glue centered on the card front.

2 Cut a 4¾" square of black paper and glue centered on the gold paper.

3 Cut a 4⁵⁄₈" square of floral paper with the deckle scissors and glue centered on the black paper.

4 Mat the rosebuds on black paper leaving a ¹⁄₁₆" border. Glue to the gold/black paper leaving a ¼" deckle border. Glue centered on the card.

Hydrangea Garden

by Lisa Garcia-Bergstedt

5"x7¼" white card
silver garden charms pack
three ¼" silver jump rings
18 galaxy seed beads
purple pressed flower
22-gauge silver wire
patterned papers: lavender moiré, purple hydrangeas
* (from the book Paper Pizazz™ Pretty Papers)*
white paper
silver pen
E-6000®
foam adhesive tape

inside

1 Glue a 4¾"x7" piece of hydrangeas paper centered on the card front. Cut a 2⅝"x4¾" piece of purple moiré paper and mat it on white paper, leaving a ¹⁄₁₆" border.

2 Cut three 6" lengths of wire. Insert a jump ring on each charm. Thread three beads, a charm and three beads on each wire length. Wrap the wire ends to the back of the moiré mat and twist to secure. Use E-6000® to secure the beads and charms in place.

3 Cut a 1⅝"x1" rectangle of white and fold in half. Use the pen to write "For You!" inside the mini card and glue a pressed flower centered on the front. Glue the mini card to the moiré mat as shown. Use foam tape to attach the moiré mat centered on the card front.

Bouquet on Burgundy

by Kelly Woodard

5"x7¼" burgundy card
flower bouquet on paper pack
message pack
tulip embossed vellum
ivory moiré patterned paper

1 Cut a 4"x6¼" piece of vellum and glue centered on the card front.

2 Glue the bouquet centered on the vellum.

3 Inside the card: Cut a 3½"x4" piece of vellum and glue centered. Cut a 3"x1½" piece of moiré and glue centered on the vellum. Glue on the message.

Message in a Bottle
by Jeanne Jacobowski

5"x7⅛" powder blue card
palm tree from bon voyage pack
glass bottle with cork pack
solid papers: white, butter yellow, powder blue, turquoise, light green
black pen

1 Tear a 4⅞"x7" piece of white paper and glue centered on the card front. Cut a 4½"x6¾" piece of yellow paper and glue centered on the card front.

2 Cut a 4¼"x6½" piece of white paper. For the sky: Tear ½"-1" strips of white, powder blue, turquoise and light green paper. Glue to the white paper as shown.

3 For the island: Tear a 4" wide half circle from yellow and glue in the middle of the card. Glue the palm tree to the island.

4 For the water: tear and glue turquoise and light green strips on the lower half of the card. Add in some white for waves.

5 Cut a ⅝"x1" piece of white paper, write the message on it and roll up. Glue it inside the bottle and glue the bottle on the water so you can read the message.

Ladybug Parade
by Donna Smith

5"x7⅛" red card
ladybugs with rhinestones pack
daisy pack
solid papers: green, blue
black pen

1 With the fold at the top, trim the card to 4¼"x5½". Open the card and mark a line from the top left corner to the bottom right corner of the card front. Cut off the left triangle.

2 Use the red triangle as a pattern to cut a triangle each from blue and green paper. Glue the green triangle to the right side of the card front, then glue the blue triangle to the left side.

3 Glue the daisy and the ladybugs to the card front as shown. Add the message with the black pen.

Friends Are Like Flowers
by Susan Cobb

5"x7⅛" white card
dark pink, light pink fabric
flowers pack
patterned papers: green/pink/
light blue plaid, white dots
on green (from the book
Paper Pizazz™ Mixing Soft
Patterned Papers)
pastel pink vellum
pens: white, silver
X-acto® knife, cutting surface

1 Glue the dots paper covering the card front.

2 Cut a 4⅜"x6⅝" piece of plaid paper and outline with the silver pen. Use the knife to cut vertically along the dark green lines between the horizontal light blue lines on each of three rows as shown. Use the silver pen to outline the cuts.

3 Cut three 4⅜"x¾" pieces of pink vellum. Outline each strip with silver pen. Weave each strip through the plaid paper and glue the ends in place. Glue centered on the dots paper. Glue the flowers to the rows as shown. Add the message with the white pen.

Four Vases
by Jeanne Jacobowski

5¼"x7⅜" white card
vases pack
four ¾" wide pressed yellow
flowers with stems pack
solid vellum: bright blue, light
green, light blue, yellow,
orange

white patterned vellum: silver
writing, gold splotches, green
floral, silver sponged
white paper
foam adhesive tape

1 Tear four 1½"x2¾" pieces of bright blue vellum. Tear a matching piece from each patterned vellum. Glue a blue vellum piece over each patterned piece. Glue to the card front as shown.

2 Glue each vase to a different color vellum and cut the vellum to match the vase shape. Leave a sliver of vellum showing above the lip of each vase. Attach to the card with foam tape.

3 Glue one flower above each vase with its stem inside the vase.

4 Print the "You're Invited" message on white paper. Cut out and glue centered below the vases.

You're Invited

Message Connections

There's no better way to send a message to a loved one than with a beautiful handmade card! All the details are crafted lovingly just for that special person. And it's easy to do when using the wonderful Card Connection message embellishments.

Some message pieces are laser cut, the intricate details bringing a sophistication to the card. To make adding your message easy, there are words on stickers—just adhere them to your design! Creating your own announcements and invitations is easy as well. Simply print your words on vellum, attach it to a backing, then dress it up. It's easy to get your message across—here are some creative ideas for terrific results!

Congratulations!

by Susan Cobb

6¼" square white card
"Congratulations" laser cut message pack
3 white tassels pack
patterned papers: lavender stripe, lavender floral
    (from the book Paper Pizazz™ Mixing Soft
    Patterned Papers)
plum pink vellum
¹⁄₁₆" circle punch
silver pen
foam adhesive tape

1 Trim card to 6" square and cover the card front with floral paper. Use the pattern on page 80 to cut the "cornice" out of stripe paper. Mat on vellum and trim the edges of the triangles to ¹⁄₁₆" and the straight sides even with the stripe paper. Punch a hole in each point and tie on a tassel.

2 Mat the message on vellum and trim a ⅛" border. Glue to the card. Cut a 6"x⅜" strip of vellum and glue to the top of the cornice. Use the silver pen to outline all of the vellum pieces. Attach the cornice to the top of the card with foam tape.

3 From the remainder of the floral paper, cut out five daisies and attach with foam tape as shown.

Love

by Kelly Woodard

5"x6½" white card
"Love" laser cut messages pack
sheer flower and butterflies pack
patterned papers: pink flowers, white dots on green (from the book Paper Pizazz™ Mixing Soft Patterned Papers)
white paper
foam adhesive tape

1 Cover the card front with white dots paper. Cut a 5¾"x4" piece of pink flower paper and mat it on white leaving a ¹⁄₁₆" white border. Glue it centered on the card.

2 Cut a 3⅞"x2½" piece of white dots paper and mat on white with a ¹⁄₁₆" border. Glue it centered on the card front.

3 Glue the "Love" message centered on the white dots paper. Attach the flowers and butterflies as shown.

Missing You
by Susan Cobb

5"x7¼" lavender card
lavender clear sticker
  message pack
patterned papers:
  lavender stripe, iris
  on lavender (from
  the book Paper
  Pizazz™ Soft Florals
  & Patterns)

lavender vellum
lavender paper
10" of ⅞" wide sheer
  lavender ribbon with
  satin edge pack
lavender ribbon
  rosebud pack
silver pen

1 Turn the card so the fold is at the top. Cut a 6¼"x4" piece of iris paper that has a prominent iris located in the center. Mat on lavender striped paper with the stripes running vertically cutting a ¼" border. Glue to the center of the lavender card.

2 Cut a 5¾"x3½" piece of lavender vellum and place over the iris paper on the card front. Cut out a 2" square in the center of the vellum over the iris. Glue the vellum centered on the card front, with the iris showing through the window.

3 Attach the sticker message to lavender paper and trim to 2½"x¾" rectangle. Glue to the card front beneath the window. Use the silver pen to outline the vellum edges and the message.

4 Tie a lavender shoestring bow and glue to the upper left corner of the message.

inside

Smile With My Heart
by Lisa Garcia-Bergstedt

5¼" square white card
sixteen ¾" wide fabric
  flowers pack
My Funny Valentine
  sentiment sticker pack
patterned paper: red floral
  collage (from the book
  Paper Pizazz™ Collage
  Papers)

white dots vellum
paper: burgundy, white
gold pen
X-acto® knife, cutting
  surface

1 Trim the card to 5" square. Cut a 4¾" square of red floral collage paper and glue centered on the card front. Use the pattern and the knife to cut the heart from the center of the card front and set aside.

2 Cut a 4¾" square of vellum and glue centered on the back of the front flap.

3 Cut a 4¾" square of burgundy paper and glue centered on the inside of the card. Glue the cut out heart from Step 1 centered on the burgundy paper. Outline the heart and burgundy square with the gold pen. Tear a 4¾"x1" strip of the checkered pattern from the collage paper and glue centered on the heart.

4 Glue the flowers to the edge of the heart on the card front. Mat the sentiment sticker on white and attach to the card overlapping the flowers.

Moon & Stars
by Susan Cobb

5"x7¼" butter yellow card
poem for son sticker message pack
patterned paper: blue/gold moon & stars
   (from the book Paper Pizazz™ Childhood
   Memories)
pale aqua paper
metallic gold thread
foam adhesive tape
black pen

1 Turn the card so the fold is at the top. Cut a 6⅞"x4½" piece of moon & stars paper and mat on aqua paper leaving a ⅛" border. Use the pattern to cut the window from the matted paper. Glue centered on the card front.

2 Glue the poem centered in the window. Outline the edge of the aqua paper and draw squiggles on the yellow with the black pen.

3 Cut two moons from the moon & stars paper. Glue one to the moon & stars paper and attach the second with foam tape on top of the first. Cut a 2" length of gold thread, fold in half and glue one end to the corner of the poem and the other in between the moons. Tie a shoestring bow out of gold thread and glue to the poem as shown.

Three Packages by Lisa Garcia-Bergstedt

5"x7¼" white card
balloon sticker messages pack
gift packages pack
patterned paper: bright spirals/
   hearts/stars (from the book
   Paper Pizazz™ Childhood
   Memories)
red paper
gold pen
X-acto® knife, cutting surface
foam adhesive tape

inside

1 Trim the card to 5" wide x 6½". Cover the card front and the inside with the spirals paper.

2 Center three 2" squares on the card front ⅛" from each side and between each square, then 1½" from the top and bottom. Cut out using the knife.

3 Cut three 1⅞"x3¾" pieces from red. Fold in half and glue one centered in each window with the fold at the top. Attach one package to each mini card with foam tape. Attach one sticker message inside each mini card.

4 Cut a 1⁷⁄₁₆"x½" piece from the window cutouts and mat on red. Trim leaving a ¹⁄₁₆" border. Attach the "Celebrate" sticker to the center. Glue centered below the middle window on the card front. Outline with the gold pen as shown.

Anniversary Invitation

by Jeanne Jacobowski

5⁷⁄₈"x8³⁄₄" gold moiré social note
5¹⁄₄"x7¹⁵⁄₁₆" vellum overlay
⁷⁄₁₆" wide gold ribbon with metallic gold edge
¹⁄₈" hole punch

Print your invitation on the overlay. Center the overlay on the social note and punch two holes 1½" apart and 1" from the top of the social note. Thread the ribbon through the holes from the front, cross in the back and thread through the holes to the front. Trim the ends at an angle.

Rehearsal Dinner Invitation

by Jeanne Jacobowski

5⁷⁄₈"x8³⁄₄" classic stripes
   social note
5¹⁄₈"x7¹⁵⁄₁₆" opal
   raindrop vellum
   overlay
feather gold cord
gold rose
¹⁄₁₆" hole punch

Print your invitation on the overlay. Center the overlay on the social note and punch two holes ½" apart and 1" from the top of the social note. Thread the ribbon through the holes from the back and tie a shoestring bow in the front. Glue the rose to the center.

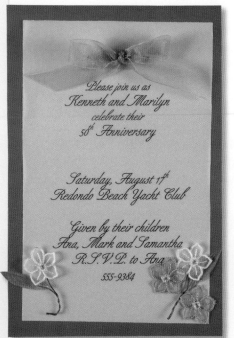

50ᵗʰ Anniversary Invitation

by Jeanne Jacobowski

5⁷⁄₈"x8³⁄₄" dark metallic gold social note
5"x7³⁄₄" vellum overlay
beaded flowers pack
15" of ⁵⁄₈" wide sheer gold ribbon
¹⁄₈" anywhere hole punch

Print your invitation on the overlay. Center the overlay on the social note and punch two holes 1" apart and 1½" from the top of the social note. Thread the ribbon through the holes from the back and tie a shoestring bow in the front. Trim the tails to 2". Attach the flowers to the bottom as shown.

25th Anniversary Invitation

by Jeanne Jacobowski

5⅞"x8¾" white swirl on silver border social note
5⅛"x8" vellum overlay
24" of ⅞" wide sheer silver ribbon
three ¼" wide pressed rosebuds with stems
⅛" hole punch

1 Print your invitation on the overlay. Center the overlay on the social note and punch two holes 1" apart and ⅝" from the top of the social note.

2 Cut the ribbon in half, layer together and use as one ribbon. Thread through the holes from the back and tie a shoestring bow in the front. Glue two rosebuds to the bottom right corner of the overlay and one to the left side.

Baby Announcement

by Lisa Garcia-Bergstedt

5⅞"x8¾" blue footprints on white social note
5½"x8⅜" vellum overlay
1½" wide sheer baby blue ribbon with striped edges
white crocheted booties pack
white paper
blue ink pad
3⁄16" hole punch

1 Print your announcement on the right side of the overlay. Ink baby's foot and press on the left side of the overlay. Center the overlay on the social note and punch two holes 1¾" apart and ½" from the top of the social note.

2 Thread the ribbon through the holes from the front, cross in the back and thread through the holes to the front. Trim the ends at an angle. Glue the booties to the ribbon.

3 Cut a white rectangle large enough to fit under the footprint. Glue to the social note centered under the footprint.

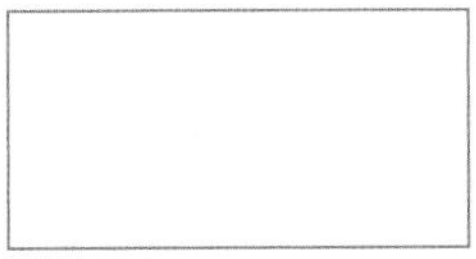

Wedding Invitation

by Susan Cobb

5⅞"x8¾" gold fleur de lis border social note
5⅛"x8" copper flecks vellum overlay
two 5" lengths of ⅝" wide sheer gold ribbon
two 5" lengths of ⅝" wide sheer gold ribbon with satin edges
white ribbon roses pack
gold pen
X-acto® knife, cutting surface

1 Print your invitation on the overlay. Use the pattern above and the knife to cut out the window from the overlay, ¾" from the bottom edge. Outline the edge of the window with the gold pen. Center the overlay over the social note and glue the top edge.

2 Layer the ribbon lengths together and make two loops with the satin edged ribbon on top. Interlock the loops and glue to the top left corner. Glue the ends to the back. Glue a ribbon rose to the center of the ribbons and another centered in the window.

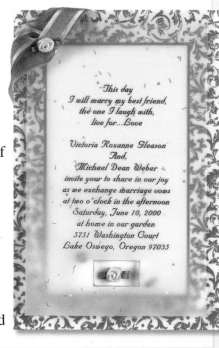

*O*nce your card has been created, it's time to turn your attention to the envelope. The first decision to make is whether you are mailing your card or presenting it in person. The postal service has certain guidelines for mailing bulky letters and cards. Consulting them may eliminate confusion when mailing your finished card (often it's as simple as writing "Fragile, please hand-stamp" on the envelope).

*D*ecorating your envelope can be almost as much fun as making your card. Of course, it's best to use flat pieces, such as stickers, seals and paper shapes, if the card is to be mailed. However,

if you plan on presenting your card in person, the envelope can be as fancy as you'd like, and the embellishments from The Card Connection are perfect for decorating it.

*T*he envelopes included with the cards in The Card Connection are large enough to allow for most embellishments you add. However, if your finished card does not fit the envelope it's very easy to make your own. Using patterned papers and vellums that coordinate with your card will add that perfect finishing touch. See page 78 for instructions on making envelopes.

Making Your Own Envelope

If, after decorating your card it's too large to fit the envelope provided, you can easily make your own from a sheet of patterned paper that coordinates with your card.

Cut a piece of patterned paper to a square–consult the table below for the appropriate size–and place it face down on the table.

Place your card face down in the center of the square, angled as shown in the diagram.

Fold in the side flaps (#1 and #2) over the back of the card and crease at the card edges. Next, fold up the bottom flap (#3) and crease. Carefully glue the bottom to the side edges where they overlap.

Remove the card from the envelope and write the recipient's name on the front. Reinsert the card, fold down the top flap (#4) and glue the edges to secure.

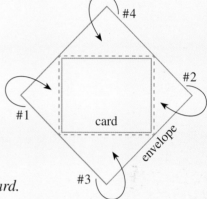

If your card is:	Then use a:
5¾"x8¾"	11¾" square
6¼" square	9" square
5¼" square	8" square
5¼"x4"	7¼" square
5"x7⅛"	9½" square
3¼"x5¼"	6¾" square

If you have a card size that is not listed, use the next size larger than your card.

On Your Wedding Day

by Susan Cobb

12"x12" square of white paper to make the envelope for a 6"x9" card
wedding cake pack
watercolor lilacs patterned paper (from the book Paper Pizazz™ Soft Florals & Patterns)
lavender vellum
22" of ⅝" wide sheer lavender ribbon with satin edge
silver pen

1 Make an envelope with the white paper following the instructions above. Cut a 7½"x6" piece of lilac paper and glue it centered on the envelope front. Trace the pattern: Fold an 8"x4" piece of paper in half; align the fold with the dotted line of the pattern and cut out. Unfold and cut from vellum. Align the long edge with the top of the envelope front as shown; glue in place.

2 Place the cake in the center of the envelope front. Wrap the ribbon around the envelope and tie in a bow, trimming the ends diagonally. Write the message and the details with the pen.

Happy Anniversary
by Susan Cobb

8½" square of white paper to make the envelope for a 5½" square card
"Happy Anniversary Mom & Dad" sticker message pack
gold fleur de lis patterned paper (from the book Paper Pizazz™ Metallic Gold)
gold paper
gold pen

1 Make an envelope with the white paper following the instructions on page 77. Cut two 2"x5½" pieces of fleur de lis paper and mat on gold. Leave a ⅟₃₂" border on the long edges and trim the short edges even with the paper. Glue one each to the top and bottom of the envelope front as shown.

2 Place the sticker in the center of the envelope front. Outline the envelope edges between the paper with the pen.

Graduation
by Shauna Berglund-Immel

5¼"x7¼" ivory envelope
graduation pack
solid papers: black, white
black pen

1 Cut a 2¼"x4" piece of white paper. Mat it on black with a narrow border.

2 Cut two 2"x2⅜" pieces of black paper. Glue all the rectangles to the envelope as shown.

3 Glue the graduation items to the envelope as shown. Use the pen to add the border and write the message.

Yellow Stripes & Daisies

by Susan Cobb

9¾" square of white vellum to make the
envelope for a 5"x7⅛" card
patterned paper: yellow stripe, yellow dots
(from the book Paper Pizazz™ Soft Tints)
white paper
1" wide pressed daisies pack
black pen

1 Make an envelope with the white vellum following the instructions on page 77. Cut a 6¾"x4½" piece of stripe paper with the stripes vertical. Mat on white paper leaving a 1/16" border. Cut a 6¾"x2" piece of dot paper and mat on white paper leaving a 1/16" border on both long sides. Glue centered on the stripe paper.

2 Cut a 2¼"x1⅜" piece of stripe paper with the stripes vertical. Mat on white leaving a 1/16" border. Glue centered on the dot paper. Glue the daisies as shown.

3 Use the black pen to write the name and address on the small stripe rectangle and "Best Wishes for a Wonderful Birthday" below the dot paper.

4 Glue the edges of the finished piece to the center of the inside front of the envelope.

back

Mother's Day

by Susan Cobb

7½" square of white paper to make the envelope
for a 5¼"x4" card
gold paper
vellum: pastel peach, embossed wild roses
two 3/16" brass eyelets
pens: brown, gold

1 Make an envelope with the white paper following the instructions on page 77. Cut a 3¾"x11" piece of roses vellum with the pattern running vertically. Wrap around the envelope as shown, overlapping the ends in the back. Crease the folds.

2 Remove the vellum wrap from the envelope. Attach the eyelets on the back to hold the ends together. Cut a 3" square of peach paper and glue centered beneath the front section of the vellum turned on point.

3 Slide the vellum wrap back onto the envelope. Cut two 1/8"x4¾" strips of gold paper. Glue to the edges of the vellum as shown. Trim the ends even with the vellum wrap. Write "Happy Mother's Day" on the front with the gold pen, then go over the letters with the black pen. Use the gold pen to add the squiggles (see pattern) to the envelope.

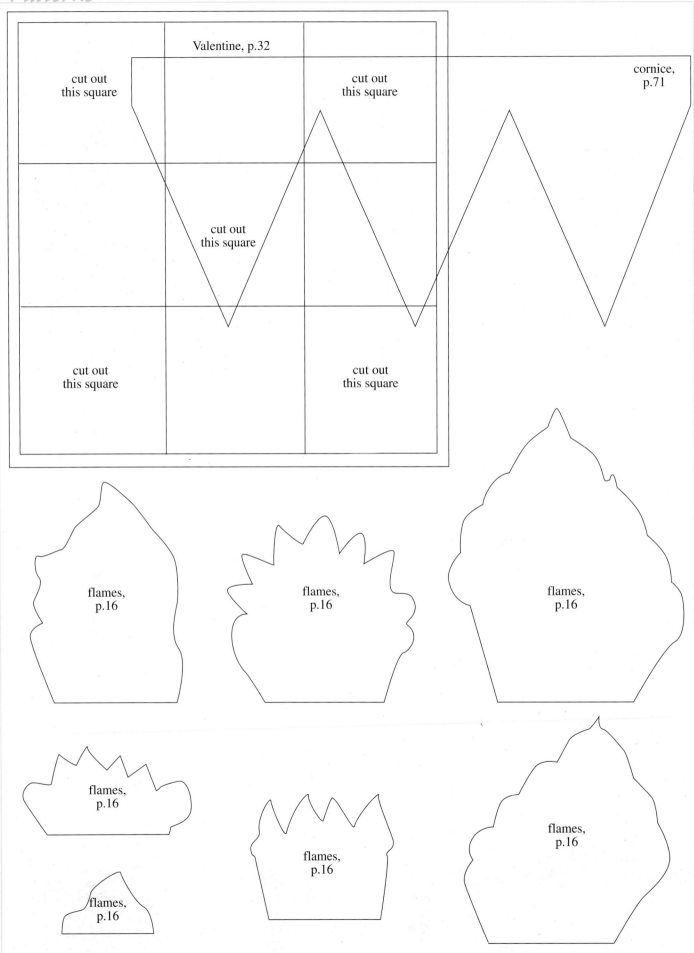

Valentine, p.32

cut out
this square

cut out
this square

cornice,
p.71

cut out
this square

cut out
this square

cut out
this square

flames,
p.16

flames,
p.16

flames,
p.16

flames,
p.16

flames,
p.16

flames,
p.16

flames,
p.16